HAND KNITTING
new directions

Alison Ellen

The Crowood Press

First published in 2002 by
The Crowood Press Ltd
Ramsbury, Marlborough
Wiltshire SN8 2HR

www.crowood.com

British Library Cataloguing-in-Publication Data
A catalogue record for this book is available from the British Library.

ISBN 1 86126 534 4

Line drawings by Annette Findlay.

Photographs by Colin Mills.

Typefaces used: M Plantin (main text and headings), Helvetica (boxed text and
labels).

Typeset and designed by
D & N Publishing
Baydon, Marlborough, Wiltshire.

Printed and bound in Malaysia by Times Offset (M) Sdn. Bhd.

CONTENTS

ACKNOWLEDGEMENTS

The network of people who have helped me with this book directly and indirectly goes back some way, firstly to teachers who inspired and developed my interest in textiles at college, at Dartington and Farnham: especially Susan Bosence, Ella McLeod and Deryn O'Connor, and the influence continues.

I could not have developed my own design business without the help of my knitters, who have tremendous skill and patience. Those who have contributed directly to this book, checking through knitting patterns and knitting the 'projects' are Joan Brown, Joan Buck, Louise Fisher, Janet Hawkins, Margaret Malony, Mary Martin and Valerie Mills. Others who have helped directly are my editor, Rachel, and Miranda who commented and improved on the text.

Items lent for the photographs were feathers supplied by Birdworld, and fleece from Joan Wigley. All knitted pieces are from the author's collection, except for those on pp.36 and 37, which belong to the artists.

Another major input comes through teaching and exploring knitting with students, which is a continuous learning process, a great way of meeting other textile enthusiasts, and has contributed enormously to helping me see how things can be explained and ideas and techniques illustrated.

Lastly, thanks to my family who have supported me throughout in every way with patience and tolerance; my parents, children, and most of all, Dan.

INTRODUCTION

Why knitting? It might be hard to imagine a creative activity that occupies no more than your personal space, makes no mess or noise, doesn't shut you away from social interaction, and can result in new clothes, accessories or furnishings. Many craft techniques involve noise or mess of some kind: at the very least they may involve banging, tapping or sanding, some use machines, others use water or create debris, so they need a special room or area to carry out. Knitting by hand has none of these disadvantages: it is not only a quiet and tidy process, but is also immensely satisfying, creative and absorbing.

Hand-knitted jumpers, and jackets in hand-dyed wool.

Samples experimenting with colour, pattern and texture, knitted with wool, silk and cotton.

Knitting is one way of making a fabric from a continuous thread, as are crochet, netting, and some forms of embroidery; therefore a very different process from the best known constructive textile technique, weaving, where two groups of threads cross and interweave at right angles to each other to create a stable, firm structured cloth.

The knitted fabric has its own individual characteristics: it is usually stretchy, and can be virtually any shape: flat, rectangular, round or tubular. Because of this versatility it can be used to make whole garments, small or large items, or furnishings. Best of all, the fabric does not need to be cut, as all the shaping can be built into the construction: whole three-dimensional items can be made, without seams.

The technique is portable, no heavy equipment is needed, it is flexible, and the creative possibilities are endless. The knitted fabric can be delicate, light and airy (as in lace knitting and shawls), heavy and warm for coats or jumpers, and either stretchy or firm. The only tools needed are knitting needles and yarn.

Historically, people often knitted out of doors, particularly in small villages and fishing communities, as it is possible to knit while walking, standing or sitting. This illustrates a flexibility that we can still take advantage of today, even though our way of life has changed so much: it can be a sociable activity, knitting while with friends, watching TV, listening to the radio, travelling by rail, plane or road.

Once a few basic stitches and different ways of constructing shapes are understood, and some basic exercises tried, opportunities for making your own designs will open up: it doesn't take long to learn and develop your skill level.

This book demonstrates some of the fundamental stitches and techniques, suggests some basic projects for clothing and for interiors, and also attempts to show the creative possibilities, encourage individual ideas, and give guidelines for translating ideas into instructions.

Traditional knitting pattern language can be inhibiting and discouraging to inventiveness, and growing up following patterns written in a variety of knitting shorthand 'codes' that appeared as pages of small print with no diagrams of shapes or construction, meant knitting blindly without really understanding the creative potential of the craft.

The approach of this book is to try to develop understanding of how knitting works, and to explore the different types of fabric produced, giving clear instructions for exercises to try, and encouraging experimentation, while always searching for the simplest, most logical way of carrying out an idea. There are stitches for making different textures with varying amounts of stretch and density: fine and lacy, thick and knobbly, or flat and firm.

ABBREVIATIONS

K	knit	yb	yarn back (to back of work)	psso	pass slip st over (over st just knitted)	dec	decrease
P	purl					inc	increase
st	stitch	yf	yarn forward (to front of work)	M1	make 1 by picking up bar bet sts (and knitting it)	rep	repeat
F	front	O	yarn over (yarn over needle in same direction as if making a st)			col	colour
B	back			K1 B	knit 1 thro back of st (this twists the st)	no	number
LH	left hand	S	slip stitch (from left to right needle, without knitting)	tog	together	cont	continue
RH	right hand			alt	alternate	bet	between
c	cable					beg	beginning

FABRIC CODING

These symbols describe the feel, drape and texture of the knitted fabric as compared with stocking stitch

> <	pulls in
^	pulls up
< >	pushes out
[ ]	thick
O	open
/	bias
∽	stretchy
–	lies flat (no curling)
|	no stretch

SYMBOLS AND ABBREVIATIONS FOR CHARTS

❙	Knit, right side rows
❘	purl, wrong side rows
━	purl, right side rows
—	knit, wrong side rows
ꝝ	knit through back of stitch
•	make one
o	yarn over needle
s	slip one
s	slip 1 with yarn in front (yarn across right side of st)
⌐	knit 2 together
⋀	slip 2 tog knitwise, K1, psso
╱	cable in front (sts cross to left)
～	cross 2, left st over right
■	plain colour stocking st for Fair Isle knitting
↯	2nd yarn carried in front of st in 2-yarn knitting

Chart patterns repeat between bold lines.

There are ways of using colour quite simply to produce rich and varied effects, and stitches for mixing colour in the knitting.

Although this book is accessible for complete beginners, it goes on to illustrate step by step the freedom afforded in knitting whole pieces, making 3-dimensional garments, cushions, and so on, by knitting in different directions. It is immensely satisfying to make a whole item or garment in one piece by knitting, so that when the last stitch is cast off, the piece is finished.

1 KNITTING TECHNIQUE

I f you take a piece of knitting and stretch it out, you can see that there is both a vertical and a horizontal nature to the structure of the fabric. The thread travels horizontally, moving up and down in continuous loops. These loops (or stitches) are formed firstly round the knitting needle, and then drop down as they pass over the new stitches on the needle, and are held securely. They then lie in vertical columns of stitches that are linked one above the other.

So as the stitch falls below the needles, the fabric is being built with a continuous thread from the bottom upwards, working either in a spiral (round and round) or back and forth (in zig-zag rows).

KNITTING NEEDLES

Knitting needles come in various forms, all useful for different aspects of knitting. They also come in a range of thicknesses (or gauges) suitable for fine or heavier yarns,

OPPOSITE PAGE:
Yarns for hand knitting.

The structure of the knitted fabric.

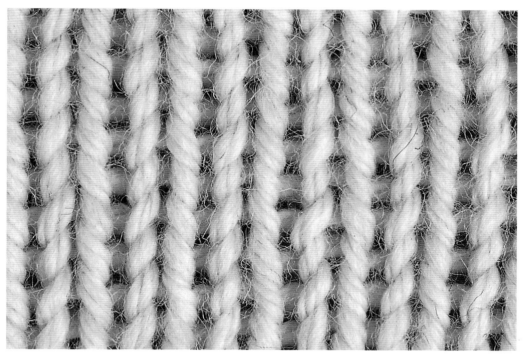

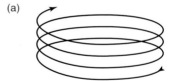

(a)   (b)

Knitting a) in the round in a spiral, b) knitting back and forth.

and the choice of size in relation to yarn will influence the closeness or openness of the fabric, and whether it feels firm or soft.

Needles are available in different materials, usually metal, but also plastics and wood or bamboo. Some people prefer working with a particular material, or find different materials more suitable according to climate or weather; hot hands make knitting difficult, and the stitches need to be able to slip easily along the needle. It is worth trying different ones to see which you find comfortable.

There are three different types of knitting needles, each with its own uses and advantages: knitting needles (sometimes called pins as they have a 'head'), circular needles, and double-ended needles.

◆ *Knitting 'pins' (or needles)* come in pairs, for knitting back and forth in rows. The head of the pin prevents the stitches falling off. These are available in different lengths and sizes, although the length may be limiting when knitting very wide items. They are probably the most commonly used knitting implements, but their use is limited to back-and-forth knitting only. Apart from familiarity, the only practical advantage of knitting on straight needles or pins over circular needles is the possibility of supporting the ends either in a knitting belt or tucked under the arm, to help bear the weight of the fabric. The needles would have pointed ends for inserting into the sheath, which would also act as a stop to the stitches. The knitting belt or knitting sheath is still in use in parts of Scotland, and became common in the nineteenth century in many rural communities because it makes it possible to knit while walking from place to place, with the result that no knitting time was wasted.

Knitting needles.

◆ *Circular needles* are designed for knitting 'in the round', making either flat circular pieces (for example, mats) or tubes. However, they can also be used for knitting back and forth by simply turning the work round or swapping the needles over at the end of the row. They have rigid needle ends for holding and working, and are joined by a flexible length of plastic for the stitches to slide along. They come in different lengths, and if you are knitting in the round, you need a length a little shorter than the circumference of the knitted piece, so the stitches have plenty of room to move sideways on the needle without being stretched.

Circular needles are the most versatile of all knitting needles:

If using them for flat (back and forth) knitting, a long circular needle makes it possible to stretch the knitting out and check the width, the design, or anything else, rather than the knitting being cramped and gathered onto a straight knitting pin. The weight distribution on a very long straight needle would not be workable, whereas on a circular needle the weight falls more centrally within the circle, onto the knitter's lap.

They also make good temporary stitch holders, as they always hang together, and so it is impossible to drop or lose a needle.

Although there are situations where it is not suitable (or is even impossible) to knit 'in the round' (*see* stripes p.78, and intarsia p.93), and there are also difficulties in knitting a circle smaller than the length of the needle, (*see* double-ended needles), there are no disadvantages to using circular needles rather than separate needles for 'back and forth' knitting.

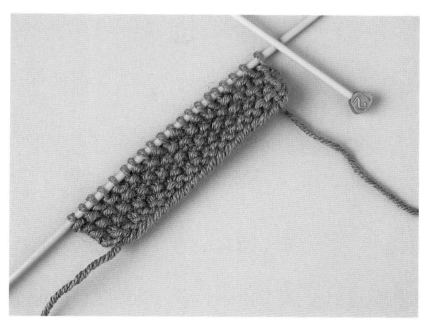

Knitting needles (or pins), knitting back and forth.

Circular needles used for knitting in the round, or back and forth.

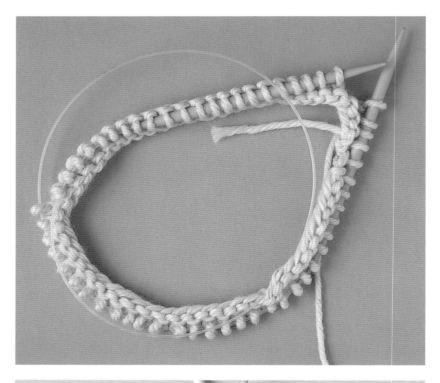

Circular needles looped to knit a circle smaller than the needle length.

- ◆ *Double-ended needles* are supplied in sets of four or five, and traditionally used for small circles with stitches distributed evenly on each needle; that is, starting at the centre of a circle in a mat, hat and so on, or for small tubes such as socks, cuffs or necks where the circumference is so small that a circular needle is not practical. Stitches can be knitted off either end of the needle, and again they come in different lengths. The main disadvantage of double-ended needles is that working in the round on several needles can be awkward and cumbersome, and can even mark the fabric with a gap or stretch at the junction of the different needles. A circular needle is therefore simpler to use if there are enough stitches.

One other use for double-ended needles working back and forth is for single-row stripes of colour, where the yarn needs to be carried up the side of the fabric. Here the stitches can be slid back along the needle to reach the yarn, and the row knitted in the same direction again. This applies equally well to knitting back and forth with circular needles.

YARNS

Any manageable yarn can be knitted, from wool, cotton or synthetics to string, rag or soft wire. It helps if the yarn is flexible, and is easier to work with if it has a little 'give' in it, but this is simply for ease of handling. For instance, wool is easier to knit with

Double-ended needles, for knitting small circles or tubes.

than cotton or linen, because it is usually slightly stretchier. This is to do with the structure of both the fibre and the yarn: different fibres have varying amounts of elasticity, and the spin and ply of the yarn also affects the stretchiness. In fact the actual process of hand knitting can soften the yarn: a fine linen or cotton may feel quite firm or hard on its cone or ball, but after being knitted the resulting fabric can feel softer and more pliable than expected.

Yarn is made from individual fibres, and it is the process of spinning that gives them the strength to hold together. If you untwist a piece of yarn and pull gently, you will see how weak it becomes without spin.

Wool, obtained by shearing sheep, is a natural animal fibre. Different breeds of sheep provide very different qualities of wool, from the fine, soft Merino to the hardy mountain breeds that have coarser, hairier wool. It also varies in character according to the age of the animal (lamb's wool is softer than sheep's), and according to the part of the body. Wool is coarsest on the animal's back and hind quarters, and softest on the underbelly.

We also use fibre from Alpacas and others in the llama family; these can make soft, heavy or light, but non-springy yarns, often with quite a limp drape, and none of the bounce of sheep's wool. Cashmere, pashmina and mohair are other well-known yarns, coming from different parts of the world from the sheep and goat families. But many other animal fibres can be spun or blended with wool, such as angora (rabbit), dog, or horse: these may not be commonly obtainable commercially, but they can be spun by hand, or bought from specialist suppliers or handspinners (enquiries to National Association of Weavers, Spinners and Dyers).

Another natural fibre obtained from an animal in a different way is silk, spun by the caterpillar of the silk moth. This varies in quality according to the breed of the moth, but also according to the processes

Double-ended needles for knitting odd-number rows of stripes.

BELOW: *Fleece from different breeds of sheep, showing variation in natural colour, length of fibre, and texture; and a spindle for hand spinning.*

A range of alpaca yarns for knitting.

involved: reeled silk is unbroken thread taken directly from the cocoon, whereas Bourette silk or silk Noile are spun mechanically from broken cocoons, and rather than having the smoothness of a continuous thread, are rougher and more textured in character. These last two silk types are considered of lower quality because of the short fibres, which means the yarn has less strength, and so they are also cheaper: however, the rough character, feel and look of this silk yarn can be attractive in its own right.

Plant fibres are different in character from animal fibres, as they do not have any elasticity or bounce, but they also have very different characteristics from each other. We know cotton and linen well, and hemp, sisal, ramie and jute perhaps less well: although not all these yarns are traditionally used in knitting, they are worth considering and experimenting with for different projects. Some fibres have a natural lustre, others are coarse and hairy, but all have different qualities of drape and weight – for example linen has a recognizable weight, handle, and tendency to crease. Nettle fibre is also used in some parts of the world, and in Nepal there has been a revival of knitting the local fibres for the tourist industry, as in the nettle fibre shawl illustrated on p.16.

When you have handled different yarns, fibres and cloths, and experimented in knitting, your awareness of the different characteristics increases, and you may find you can begin to recognize individual qualities by sight, and even identify the fibres used in fabrics and clothing in paintings, particularly the detailed paintings of the Dutch

Silk yarns: spun silks have a rougher texture than reeled silk.

and other European schools where textiles were painted so accurately.

Yarns for knitting are usually plied. This is because the single spun thread is not very strong, and can create problems when knitted, as anyone who has used handspun yarn will know. If there is a high amount of twist, the single thread can behave with a mind of its own and force the knitted fabric to lean in a diagonal direction, which is impossible to correct even by pressing or stretching. Plying threads, which means twisting two, three or four together in the opposite direction to the spin, will counteract this tendency, creating a stable, balanced yarn, and also give added strength.

In commercial knitting yarns, the thickness is described by the number of plies, so for instance 4-ply is a more or

ABOVE: Linen yarns, and knitted pieces in fine and heavier linen.

LEFT: Cotton and cotton/linen mix yarns and knitting.

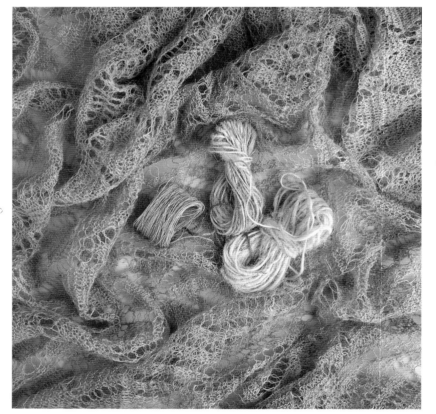

ABOVE LEFT: Contemporary examples of knitting in plant fibres, sisal washing mitts bought in Greece and England, knitted in China.

ABOVE: Knitting with jute 'string'.

less standard weight or thickness, whether it is wool, cotton or any other fibre. However, if you experiment with spinning your own yarns, or with buying yarn from companies that also supply for weaving and other textile techniques, you will find that it is important to know the 'count' or reference for the thickness of the particular thread as well as the number of plies: that is, you might find a 4-ply of very fine counts is finer than a 2-ply weaving yarn of chunkier threads.

This need not be a problem. The only important factor is to understand the

Shawl knitted in Nepal from 'Allo' fibre (Girardinia diversifolia).

relationship of yarn to needle size, and the tension of the knitting, that is, how many stitches there are to a given measurement, when knitted up. Most knitting yarns give suggested needle sizes, and if you experiment a little, you will see what size suits which yarn for your purpose.

In the past, fine yarns were used more commonly, in fact 4-ply knitting yarn was possibly the thickest yarn available until the 1950s. Some of the finest wool used was in Shetland shawls, which were traditionally knitted in a hand-spun singles yarn, spun with hardly more than one fibre's thickness. There are examples in collections in Britain, worth searching out, as they have to be seen to appreciate the delicacy of the spinning and the knitting. This use of a singles yarn shows an exception to the rule regarding the necessity of plying: if the fibre is long enough, and the amount of spin is enough to give strength without being enough to twist the fabric, it is possible to knit with, but plied yarn is stronger and more even, and singles yarns are not usually produced commercially.

Other examples of fine knitting can be seen in cotton and linen table mats and bedspreads made in the late nineteenth and early twentieth centuries. They represent hours of work, but have a wonderful drape and weight because of the fine gauge. It is worth looking in antique shops (usually among the 'lace' items) and asking in local museums if they have any examples, as pieces are sometimes kept in store and not always displayed.

Thicker yarns were introduced throughout the twentieth century, as we became more impatient and time-conscious, wanting quick results and a thicker, heavier look. Now the most commonly available knitting yarns are 'double knitting' and 'chunky' wools and synthetics rather than 2- and 4-ply; and there is a wide range of 'fancy' yarns with textured spins and random colouring. These are good for making even a simple plain knitted stitch look interesting.

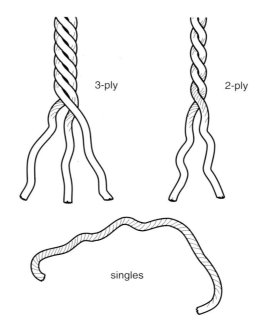

'Singles' and plied yarns.

However, if you find the yarns available to you boring or expensive or limited in colour, and would like to experiment and make more individual designs, it is not difficult to find alternative materials to knit with. Strips of cloth can be used, that is, 'rag' knitting; also string, ribbon, metal or any strip of material that can be handled.

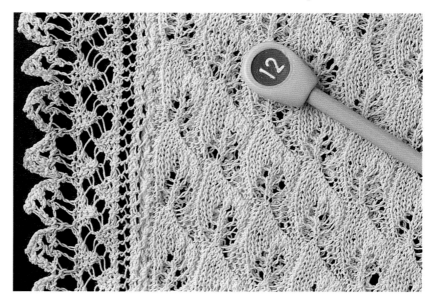

Early twentieth-century very finely knitted cotton lace 'pocket'.

Wool and cotton cloth cut into bias strips for knitting.

BELOW: Crochet, showing the way the loops interlink across each other, making a firm, non-stretchy fabric.

THE KNITTED FABRIC

The characteristic that makes knitting so different from woven and most other fabrics is its stretch. This can be varied by using different stitches, but in the most commonly used knitting stitch, stocking stitch, the fabric will stretch in all directions: vertically, diagonally, but most of all sideways. If you look at the shape of the knitted stitch in a piece of plain stocking stitch knitting, it is wider than it is tall, being interlinked in a flowing, uninterrupted motion, unlike crochet where the loop is locked over the neighbouring loop in both directions, preventing movement.

The reason for analysing the structure of knitting in detail is that the more you can understand about how it is formed, the more potential there is for innovative ideas and designs. It also helps you make the right decisions in choosing the most suitable yarns and stitches for each project. Understanding grows gradually with experience, but looking at examples and illustrations, and analysing and questioning all help to speed up the process. It can be enlightening and inspiring to look at pieces of knitting and at books from the past with an enquiring mind and imagination – for example, could a particular stitch be used in clothing instead of in a tea cosy? Perhaps the shaping of a pleated skirt could be used to form a cushion or as a throw?

The height of skill in the technique of hand knitting was probably reached before the middle of the twentieth century, partly because there was not a great choice of yarns for knitting, so the use of the technique was more inventive than later on when more fancy yarns were introduced and provided instant interest and decoration. As we reached the second half of the twentieth century, the combination of a fashion for simple, loose shapes and the desire for instant results meant that there was a dumbing-down of technique, and textured, heavier coloured yarns provided the interest. Earlier, decoration was produced by using different stitches, and a desire for tailored shaping meant a creative and skilled use of stitches. Searching for, looking at and questioning the structure of earlier examples of knitting can spark off ideas for contemporary ways of using stitches.

KNITTING SHAPES

One of the great advantages of knitting is that every edge of a piece of knitted fabric is a selvedge: no cutting is required and each border is immediately a finished edge.

There is no limit to the variety of shapes that can be knitted by hand, except the size and weight that can be handled, so the scope for creating shapes and designs is enormous.

Flat Pieces

The simplest and most obvious shape is a rectangle or square, and the simplest way of knitting it is with a bottom (cast on) edge, two side edges and a top (cast off) edge. However, there are more inventive ways of constructing such a simple shape without leading to anything too complicated. Try and think of alternative ways of knitting a square, and this may lead to new design ideas (*see* Chapter 3).

Circles and ovals can be knitted, either growing outwards from the centre, or inwards from the outside edge; in both these cases the increasing and decreasing takes place within the circle. Or you can work round sideways in linked sections, or begin with a few stitches at the edge as if knitting a square, shaping through increasing and decreasing at the edges.

Following on from this, random shapes could be constructed in similar ways: upwards, downwards, sideways, from the centre, from the edge – there are endless possibilities.

Tubes

Tubes can be knitted in any width from two, three or four stitches or more: from the bottom upwards, either on a group of double-ended needles, or circular needles.

To knit a simple 2-stitch cord, use two double-ended needles, and always knit the two stitches from the same end of the needle. Where the yarn is carried across at the back, it will pull the stitches magically into a cord.

To make larger cords or small tubes, use two stitches per needle, making a total of six stitches on three needles, or eight stitches on four needles. Use more stitches according to the size you want. Again, tubes need not be cylindrical, but can be shaped by increasing and decreasing.

Knitting a variety of shapes and directions.

Circle knitted from the centre.

It is possible to be freely creative, working without planning in an organic way, or to be more regimented with calculations worked out accurately first. The best combination may be to work out a plan in advance, but to be ready to vary the plan as it takes shape, and as more ideas form during the making. For example, if unexpected things happen, it may be that more ideas will arrive by questioning, and discovering what the fabric wants to do naturally rather than trying to dictate a shape or behaviour that fights against the tendency of the knitting.

It is good to have a free, experimental and adventurous approach, but there has to be a practical level too: if an apparently random construction of knitting in different directions is to look purposeful and professional, the tension of the knitting will have to be worked out first, as different numbers of stitches are needed according to the direction of the knitting.

For instance, if you have knitted a square, and want to pick up stitches along the side to knit another square at right angles, you will find that because the knitted stitch is wider than it is tall, there are more rows than stitches in your square, so less stitches need to be picked up from the side than the number of rows. This can be worked out beforehand (*see* Chapter 5).

You can pick up stitches from anywhere on the surface of the knitting to make textured or sculptural pieces, or functional pieces such as straps, ties or pockets.

There is also a way of knitting back and forth on a group of stitches on straight needles as if knitting ordinary rows, but knitting and slipping alternate stitches, making a 'double cloth' that can open into a tube, but working from a straight base (*see* p.73).

DIFFERENT DIRECTIONS

Stitches can be picked up from any edge, or from the surface of knitting. A piece can grow outwards from a central point by picking up stitches from the sides or the bottom edge, to make organic or geometric shapes. This could be done in flat knitting or tubular, shaped or straight.

STITCHES

The way the knitted loops are made on the needle and the way they are dropped off the needle can be varied, influencing the sort of fabric produced. Both the loops on the needle and these variations are referred to as 'stitches', for example 'stocking stitch' or 'moss stitch'. Different arrangements of stitches produce different amounts of thickness and stretch, and of course different textures and patterns.

Knitted tubes: 2-stitch, 4-stitch, 12-stitch, and a tube shaped by increasing and decreasing.

Picking up stitches from the side edge.

(a)

(b)

(c)

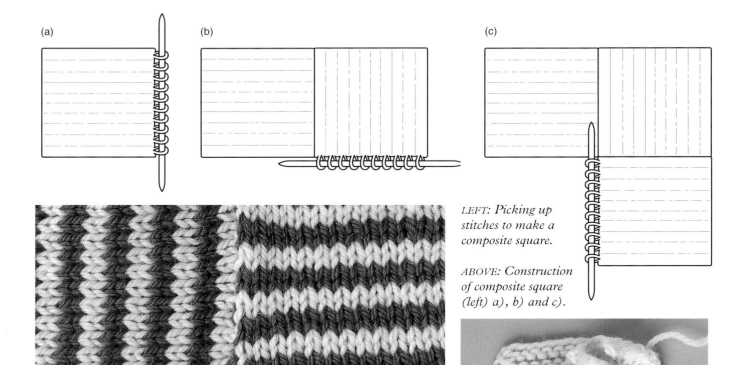

LEFT: Picking up stitches to make a composite square.

ABOVE: Construction of composite square (left) a), b) and c).

RIGHT: Picking up stitches from the surface of the knitting.

These are the two basic ways of forming the loop (stitch) from which the majority of stitches are composed:

◆ 'Knit'(or 'plain') stitches. With these, the yarn is placed round the needle from front to back, and the stitch slipped off so that the loop falls to the back of the work.

KNITTING BACK AND FORTH

a) garter st ^ [ ] ⌣ –
   Knit every row

b) stocking st
   Row 1) knit
   Row 2) purl

c) moss st ^ < > –
   uneven no of sts
   Row 1) K1, P1
   Row 2) K1, P1

d) ribbing > < [ ] ⌣ –
   even no of sts
   Row 1) K1, P1
   Row 2) K1, P1

e) double moss st – even no of sts
   Row 1) K2, P2
   Row 2) K2, P2
   Row 3) P2, K2
   Row 4) P2, K2

f) 5-st squares –
   Row 1) P5, K5: the same in the round. Work each block of 5 sts
   in stocking st (and reverse stocking st) for 6 rows, then swap over.

KNITTING IN THE ROUND

Knit one round, purl one round

Round 1) knit
Round 2) knit

Round 1) K1, P1
Round 2) P1, K1

Round 1) K1, P1
Round 2) K1, P1

Round 1) K2, P2
Round 2) K2, P2
Round 3) P2, K2
Round 4) P2, K2

LEFT: *Knit and purl patterns, 10 rows of each separated by stocking stitch: starting from the bottom, garter st, moss st, 1+1 ribbing, double moss st, checkerboard.*

Charts for these sts.

(a)
(b)
(c)
(d)
(e)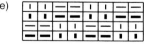
(f)

If working in the round, the result is stocking stitch, with all loops falling to the reverse side of the fabric. This is the most widely used stitch, having a characteristically smooth front formed by the vertical sides of the loops, and a rougher textured back, formed by the horizontal top of the loop.

If working back and forth, the work is turned at the end of each row, so the loops fall on alternate sides of the fabric in ridges, making 'garter stitch'.

◆ Purl stitches are the reverse of knit: yarn travels round the needle from the back to the front, and the stitch slips off towards the knitter, at the front of the fabric. The same applies as above with regard to

knitting in the round when the stitches will always fall to the front, making 'reverse side' stocking stitch. If knitting back and forth, again continuous purl stitches will fall to alternate sides of the fabric, making garter stitch.

◆ So: in order to make garter stitch when knitting back and forth, knit or purl every row.

◆ To make garter stitch when knitting in the round, do alternate rounds of plain and purl.

◆ To make stocking stitch when knitting back and forth, do alternate rows of plain and purl.

◆ To make stocking stitch when knitting in the round, knit or purl every round.

This may sound obvious, and will be if you are used to knitting in the round: the point is to understand why it happens, and to be able see and to control any mistakes.

The follow-on logic from this is to see that if you are working in the round, but following instructions for a particular stitch that is most likely to be written for back and forth knitting, then all knits and purls have to be reversed on alternate rounds, which in the instructions would be the 'wrong-side' rows.

If knit and purl stitches are grouped within each row and worked in repeats, textured patterns are made. These will show most successfully in plain yarns and a firm tension (*see* page 23).

KNITTING TECHNIQUE

Advice was sometimes given in early articles on knitting concerning style and method, but there are no absolute rules. The basic actions involve holding the needles, holding the yarn and placing it round the needle, then slipping the stitch off the needle. As knitting has been passed on mainly by word of mouth (or hand) for generations, for all these actions there are many different styles and methods, often differing by region. People usually stay with the way they have learnt from childhood and, if they knit a lot, will have developed a good speed. However, it is really worth questioning the way you knit, for these reasons: do you feel tense when knitting? Do your neck or shoulders ache, or do you get headaches? Is your knitting loose or tight? Do you find that you knit slowly or unevenly?

These are all common problems that highlight how difficult it is to change a habitual way of knitting. It used to be a sociable activity, with exchange of ideas and methods. It would have been obvious within a group who had the most efficient technique, and advice could have been exchanged. However, as we knit mostly in isolation now, there is not so much opportunity to look at our knitting methods objectively.

It is so much easier to learn in childhood, and children would have been constantly guided in families and groups. Now it is quite likely that a method of knitting will be learnt from a book, perhaps partly understood, and quickly become a habitual way of working, with no friendly comments on hand to improve the action.

It is possible to change and improve your method, but you have to want to do it! It needs a huge effort, with lots of patience, and some practice every day until it becomes automatic. So it is essential first to see the point of changing an old way of working: for instance that it will make your knitting much faster, more comfortable, more even, or all of these.

Although there has been debate and discussion in knitting magazines on ways of holding wool and needles, it is the absolute basics that you need to question: the main aim is to try to knit as comfortably and efficiently as possible. Hand knitting is not a particularly speedy technique, so it seems sensible to make it as easy and economical as you can, with no extra movements that aren't strictly necessary.

These are some guidelines:

◆ Sit comfortably, and consciously relax your shoulders and neck, at frequent intervals.

◆ Holding the needles on top, not like a pencil, means that your fingers are closer to the tips of the needles without being hampered by the knitted fabric, and can move around more freely with less distance to carry the yarn.

◆ Holding the yarn over the tip of your first finger also means it is as near the point of the needle as possible, with

Knitting with yarn in one hand.

one twist round the little finger keeping it under tension.

With these two finger positions, in practice it is absolutely unnecessary to take your hand right off the needle while putting the yarn round the needle: it is a waste of both time and energy, the movement needs to be as small and efficient as possible.

Knitting stitches are usually carried on the left-hand needle, and knitted onto the right-hand needle. However, it is equally possible to knit from right needle to left, as many left-handed knitters have learnt to do by sitting opposite their teacher and copying in mirror image. But as all books and instructions will show the usual left-to-right method, that is the way described here. If you learn both methods, it is possible to knit backwards and forwards from left to right needle, and right to left without having to turn the knitting: that is, to make stocking stitch, it becomes unnecessary to purl: this is particularly useful if you are working backwards and forwards on a small group of stitches, for instance in entrelac knitting, or making bobbles (*see* figures on pp.63 and 65).

The yarn, however, can be held in the right or the left hand to achieve the same result. If you can learn to use either hand, it will speed up the process enormously when knitting with two colours, as one can be held in each hand (*see* p.90).

Children can be taught to knit from the age of five or six, and a good way to start is to sit them on your knee when small enough, let them hold the needles and put the needle into the stitch, but begin by putting the yarn round the needle for them. When asked to pick up the yarn themselves, they will as often use the left hand as the right, even if right-handed. There is an argument in favour of left-handed (sometimes called 'Continental') knitting, as there is a shorter journey round the needle, particularly for knit stitches, and therefore it is quicker. There is no need to be bound by convention: it doesn't matter which hand you use as long as you follow the aim of knitting as comfortably and efficiently as possible.

2 A BRIEF HISTORY OF KNITTING

Looking at knitting from the past is enormously constructive, as again it provokes more questioning and analysing, and leads to better understanding of the technique and its possibilities. In many ways our mass-produced household items of today, clothes, tools and utensils, look so much slicker and more professional than items from the past, that we can be misled into thinking that everything used to be cruder and more roughly made, but if we consider the creative process involved in hand crafts, this is absolutely not the case. It is often inspiring to look at the skill and detail involved in all crafts, and if we look at knitted pieces carried out as recently as fifty years ago in a less hurried world, the work was often very much finer and more intricate than we would consider making today.

Naturally textiles have not survived over the years as well as the 'hard crafts' of pottery, wood, stone or metal, but there are some surprisingly ancient pieces in existence, often hundreds of years old. Some textiles and clothing have been preserved in exceptionally dry conditions and others were waterlogged but preserved in acid conditions, for example in the 'bog burials' in Denmark. Frequently pieces of different fabrics have been found that may look like knitting, but are not always constructed by the hand-knitting technique as we know it now. Some textile pieces found in Peru that have the appearance of knitting, dating from as far back as 400BC, when analysed, reveal that although the fabric looks superficially like knitting, the structure is slightly different in that the stitches are twisted, and must have been made with a needle and thread rather than on knitting needles. However, garments and fragments from Egypt dated to the fifth century AD (Rutt, 1987) are thought to be the earliest examples of 'real' knitting.

'Needle knitting'.

OPPOSITE PAGE:
Cotton mats and edgings in 'lace' sts.

It is easy to imagine that both knitting and crochet would have developed from 'playing' with thread; looping, knotting, pulling one loop through another, eventually finding that the loops could be built up one after another to make a continuous structure. At first, the yarn might have been pulled through with fingers or a hook, then with a sewing needle, possibly with short lengths of yarn being more readily available, but eventually the method evolved into pulling a continuous thread through loop-by-loop with a knitting needle (or pin).

Hooked as well as straight needles have been found in different parts of the world, suggesting an early relationship with crochet and have been used until recently in parts of Portugal and Peru. There is also a technique still used in parts of the world sometimes called Tunisian crochet, or 'Tricot', which uses a hooked needle to alternately knit and crochet off a row of stitches. Links like this between techniques help to illustrate the spread of knitting throughout the world. The earliest examples that are definitely made in the technique we now know as hand knitting were found in Egypt, and later in parts of southern Europe. From here it spread north and east throughout Europe to reach Britain in Tudor times, then from Spain and Portugal it travelled with early explorers across to South America, where there are still similarities in the knitting methods, such as wrapping the yarn round the back of the neck to give tension and leave the hands free to manoeuvre the needles.

Countries in Eastern Europe and Scandinavia adopted the technique willingly to make warm woollen clothing, often very colourful and decorative, and developed their own variations. One example that may have either grown out of colour knitting or preceded it is the two-yarn knitting of Sweden, where by alternating two yarns (often of the same colour) a thicker fabric was formed, and by carrying the second yarn in different formations on the front of the work, textured patterns could be made that have a different character from commoner single-yarn stitch patterns.

In the Middle Ages in Europe there was a method of making knitted carpets thought to have been constructed on peg frames. They are wonderfully rich and ornately patterned, and although the fabric could have been hand knitted, presumably the frame was a solution to the problem of handling the weight that large pieces would have entailed. This early frame is an example of the idea that developed later into the knitting machine, where each stitch was held on a separate peg and new stitches made by manoeuvring the stitch off the peg, firstly by hand, and much later, when the latched hook was invented, mechanically. Other examples of hand frames remain from the nineteenth and twentieth centuries: at the simplest level as the 'knitting Nancy' or wooden doll with four pegs or staples in the top and a hollow centre, where the yarn is lifted by hand over each peg, and a narrow 4-stitch cord appears through the base of the doll. This was developed into a more mechanized device with proper latched hooks instead of pegs, and a small handle to wind that rotates and moves the hooks to make the stitches: in effect just like an early knitting machine. There were also large simple peg frames that would knit a tube large enough for a garment, but the action of making stitches is clumsier and more difficult to control than hand knitting on needles, and probably not a great advance in the development of the machine.

Some of the first hand-knitted garments were socks, sometimes with a separated toe, as the fifth-century example from Egypt mentioned earlier shows. Knitting socks spread gradually throughout Europe and eastwards, becoming absorbed into regional dress along with variations such as

Tunisian crochet or 'tricot': this is called by various names, and combines knitting and crochet.

SCANDINAVIAN 2-YARN KNITTING [ ].

This produces a very thick, warm knitted fabric, and even though 2 yarns of the same colour are used, patterns can be produced by carrying the yarns in front of the stitches.

For plain stocking stitch fabric, use 2 separate yarns to knit (or purl) alternate stitches.

HORIZONTAL RIDGES
Work one or more rows in stocking stitch: with knit side facing, bring both yarns to the front and work a purl row. Alternatively, with purl side facing, take both yarns back and work a knit row.

PATTERN MOTIF
This motif is worked over 2 rows, and the yarn crosses in front of single stitches, alternating in the second row.
Row 1) right side: work in knit to st before centre of motif, bring yarn used for the st before last to the front, and use it to P1. Keeping this yarn at the front, use the yarn still at the back to knit the next st, then P1 again with the yarn at the front, and pass it through to the back. Continue knitting row.
Row 2) Purl to the st before the centre of motif. Pass the yarn used for the last st back to the right side, use the yarn still on the wrong side to purl the next st, K the next st with the yarn at the right side and leave it there; then P1 with yarn at the wrong side, bring back the yarn from the right side to wrong side, and continue purling row.

This motif can be grouped in different ways, including the one below:

CHECKERBOARD PATTERN
Worked on stitches divisible by 6.
Row 1) *K3, bring yarn from the st before last to right side and P1, leaving yarn forward. K1 using back yarn, P1 with front yarn, and take it back. Rep from * to end.
Row 2) *take yarn from st before last back to right side, and leave it. P1 using wrong-side yarn, K1 using right-side yarn, and leave it there, P1 using wrong-side yarn, and bring back right-side yarn to wrong side. P3, rep from * to end.
Row 3) * bring yarn from st before last st to right side and P1, leaving it at front. K1 with wrong-side yarn, P1 with front yarn and take it back, K3, rep from * to end.
Row 4) * P3, take yarn from last st to right side leaving it, P1 with wrong-side yarn, K1 with right-side yarn leaving it there, P1 with wrong-side yarn, bring right-side yarn to wrong side, rep from * to end.
  Rep these 4 rows for a textured checkerboard pattern, alternating the squares on the next 4 rows.

Chart for 2-yarn knitting.

the tubular leg pieces and armbands knitted in Greece and Albania, that were often highly patterned. The shaping of the socks was often a simple tube, with the heel worked last. A slit would be left for the heel, and the foot knitted on, culminating in a toe shaped by decreasing on either side of the foot to make a point. The stitches would then have been picked up around the heel slit, and another 'toe' shape made, resulting in a pointed heel. Although the shape is not as tailored and detailed as later more complex sock heels, the stretchy character of the fabric makes it a strong but

simple wearable shape. Mary Thomas referred to this heel in her books of the 1930s in a way that today sounds to us rather patronizing, as a 'peasant heel'.

Hand knitting took a leap forward in fineness and complexity in sixteenth-century Britain with the appearance of knitted stockings for the aristocracy. These must have been a huge improvement over the woven cloth hose worn previously, that often needed to be cross-gartered to hold them up. The stretchy knitted fabric must have had great advantages in fitting and comfort: we take 'jersey' fabric so much

Peg dolls for knitting cords.

BELOW: '*Knitting Nancy*'.

BELOW RIGHT: Latched '*machine*' *for knitting cords.*

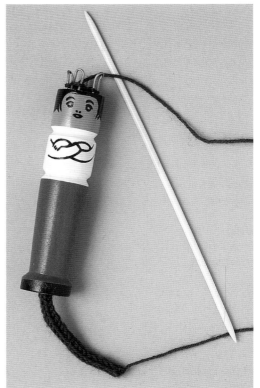

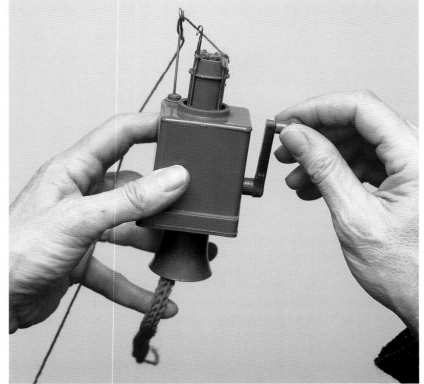

for granted now, that it is hard to imagine a world without it, when all shaping had to be skilfully inserted by cutting and sewing into woven materials. We can see examples of Tudor stockings in the Victoria and Albert Museum in London showing detailed shaping around the calf and ankle, and a more sophisticated turned heel than the one described above. At the same time as fine silk stockings were made for the king and nobility, there also developed a large industry in woollen stocking production with centres all over Britain, where wool was distributed to hand knitters and stockings were collected at central towns, well into the nineteenth century.

Other knitted garments from the sixteenth century include hats that were knitted and then felted and blocked into shape, which is one example of a widely used practice of felting knitting. The basic knitted structure gives strength and the slightly stretchy character to the fabric even after felting, which makes it comfortable to wear. There are knitted and felted Tudor hats from Britain still surviving in museums, but this technique was probably used widely for hats, such as the beret, and the north African 'fez' or cap. It was also used for other clothing such as traditional jackets and coats in Austria, which are still felted from knitted cloth today.

Garments that survive from the seventeenth century are silk 'shirts' or 'vests' such as the famous knitted shirt worn by Charles I at his execution, which is in the collection at the Victoria and Albert Museum, London. This is a beautifully fine piece of knitting with intricate patterning in plain and purl stitches in coloured silk yarns, but with surprisingly long floats of yarn on the reverse. It had a square construction, that is, no body shaping, straight shoulder join, and straight armholes. Apart from hats, knitted clothes were mostly undergarments at this time, but the basic rectangular 'shirt' or 'vest' construction must have been handed down through to the nineteenth century

when outer garments began increasingly to be knitted, as the same form can be seen in fishermen's ganseys of the twentieth century that were made all round the coast of Britain. Outer garments had a different purpose and requirement from the fine undervests and shirts of earlier centuries, and so were knitted in warm and weatherproof wool, in a firm tension.

There are several books recording Gansey (or Jersey and Guernsey) knitting around the coasts of Britain, and as there are examples on show in museums, we can admire the fine knitting, often 5-ply wool worked on needles size 2¼mm (13); and the imaginative use of the plain and purl stitch to create a huge variety of patterning, that also had the function of making thicker, warmer areas over the back and chest of the fisherman.

Details of socks from Eastern Europe to the Himalayas, showing different methods of turning heels, including the simple pointed heel.

After the Industrial Revolution and the invention of the first stocking-knitting machines, the cottage industry of hand knitting stockings and other items declined, but people kept knitting for their own use and pleasure. Regional styles had grown up around Britain, with the Scottish Isles developing coloured and patterned clothing in Fair Isle and Shetland, using hand-spun wool dyed at first mostly in natural dyes to give a range of soft, sympathetic colours, including some surprisingly bold reds. The patterns were usually geometric in fairly small repeats, and even though the overall effect could be very colourful, with colours frequently changing throughout a garment, they never used more than two colours in each row of knitting.

Shetlanders also became well known for 'lace' shawls, knitted from extremely finely spun single wool thread; there are examples still existing of the famous lace patterned shawls that were so fine they could be pulled through a wedding ring. Babies' socks and dresses were also knitted in this delicate lacy knitting.

Ireland developed a style later known as 'Aran', using plain (often white or undyed) wool and heavily textured stitches including cables and cross-over stitches in vertical panels, often many different patterns on one garment, making jumpers that were not only intricate and decorative, but very warm.

In Victorian society, women knitted as a social pastime, both clothing and fine cotton mats and bedspreads for their homes. European wars at the end of the nineteenth and beginning of the twentieth centuries gave women an added purpose in knitting useful items for men such as gloves, balaclavas, socks and stockings.

From the 1920s, fashion began noticeably to influence knitting design, and perhaps knitted garments influenced fashion. Jumpers and cardigans became everyday items of clothing, and luckily for us, instructions and patterns began to be printed and published, so we have good evidence in surviving knitting books and patterns of the styles that were popular.

From this time through to the 1940s and 50s there were lots of patterns for babies: hats, bonnets, socks, leggings, jackets, vests and cot blankets. Older children also wore hand-knitted socks, vests, knickers, jumpers and swimsuits, as well as hats and gloves, and there are patterns that reveal a lot about our social history, showing how children were expected to turn into adults overnight, with no styles for teenagers, but 'young men' and 'young women'.

For men there were Fair Isle jumpers, cabled jumpers for cricket, stockings for wearing with knee breeches or kilts, gloves, scarves and hats, and even ties and braces. For a while for women there were patterns for almost every item of clothing: everything from bras and knickers to bed-jackets; also evening wear, and fitted dresses and pleated skirts, as well as fitted jumpers and cardigans, hats, gloves and scarves.

More items began to be knitted for use in the home: cotton was available for knitting as well as wool, and there are patterns for cotton bathmats in a looped stitch giving a shaggy pile, oven cloths and dish cloths in cotton. Finer quality cotton was used for table mats, antimacassars for chair backs, both of which were often knitted in lacy stitches, and sometimes mistakenly described as 'lace', and confused with bobbin and other methods of lace making rather than knitting. Bedspreads were also knitted, usually in units such as squares or diamonds in heavily textured stitches, which could then be stitched or crocheted together. A knitted cotton bedspread from the early twentieth century had a wonderful individual weight and drape quite different from a woven bedspread, and characterized by the fineness of the knitting.

Before the invention of the tea bag, tea cosies were used to keep the teapot warm while the tea brewed. Tea cosies were made usually in wool for warmth, with special stitches developed for their heat-trapping qualities. They could also often be decorative or whimsical.

Cushion covers were also knitted, and there are knitting patterns and illustrations surviving showing imaginative construction for circular cushions as well as bolsters and rectangular shapes.

Throughout the 1960s and 70s the emphasis changed again, as gradually it became cheaper to buy ready-made jumpers, but patterns for baby clothes continued to be popular, especially dresses, jackets, hats and leggings, until the invention of easy-care baby-grows. For adults, beginning in the 1960s, there was a fashion for heavy, chunky, big, loose jumpers, which also coincided with the desire for instant results and quick production, and as at this time most people still learnt to knit, it was a common sight to see people knitting, even in public. There are films and TV programmes from the 1960s showing teenage

ABOVE: *Knitting books published 1900–1950.*

LEFT: *Patterns and instructions from early twentieth-century knitting books.*

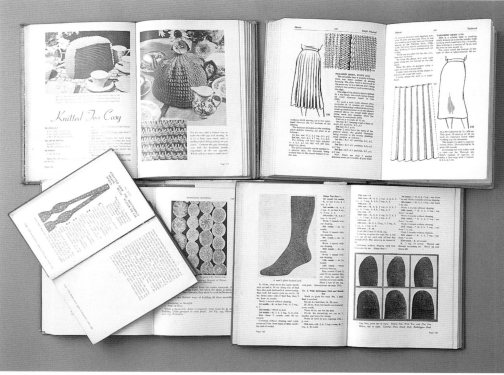

ABOVE: *Cotton mats and chair backs from the first half of the twentieth century: the mat in front knitted in double moss stitch.*

ABOVE RIGHT: *Early twentieth-century cotton bedspread.*

girls sitting and gossiping together with their knitting. It was not unusual to see people knitting on trains, in waiting rooms, bus stops, and anywhere there was time to sit down.

However, the beginning of a big change occurred at around this time, as the teaching of knitting and other needlework was dropped from the school curriculum (in England earlier than Scotland or Ireland) and together with a growing emphasis on quick results, a fast fashion turnover and buying cheaper clothes, there was a lull in knitting, and consequently a gradual decline in shops supplying knitting yarns

By this time people were used to knitting only with written instructions rather than the earlier method of word of mouth and discussion. In retrospect this has turned out to be inhibiting to any creativity or understanding of the possibilities of hand knitting. However, there was a change in the 1980s with a new emphasis on simply

shaped garments and colour and pattern in knitting. With the influence of new designers such as Kaffe Fassett and a new drive towards individual creativity, the restrictions of written knitting patterns began to be shaken off. The idea grew that anything was possible: colours could be used in abundance with no rules, and the patterns could sweep freely across garments in ways not seen before.

Another influence growing at the same time, that has continued to develop over the last twenty years or more, has been an enormous expansion in travel around the world to areas not previously intruded on by tourism. With this, an interest has grown in traditional crafts from different communities. Hand-made items from different places began to be imported, including knitted clothes such as jumpers, hats and socks from the South American countries. With the added input of books and television programmes, all this has opened our eyes to different styles, methods and patternings that have gradually become incorporated into new fashions in knitting. As many ethnic styles of knitting are based on very simple, untailored shapes, it has been an easy way for non-knitters to be introduced to the technique, knitting uncomplicated square and rectangular garments, and creating colour and pattern with different yarns.

Throughout the 1980s new designers appeared, producing individual hand- and machine-knitted garments, with the emphasis broadly on colour and pattern.

It becomes difficult to look back objectively as we get closer to the present, but there has been a gradual decline in the prestige of knitting as a pastime or as a creative textile technique, compared with, for example, weaving, stitching, or perhaps felting. This has to be due in part to the fact that young people are no longer encouraged to knit; it has became associated with something that only old people do, and this has led to its loss of energy and charisma.

However, a few individual knitting designers carried on through the 1990s, with new interest growing in shaping and finishing the cloth, for example the growth of preoccupation with felted cloth, especially in machine knitting. There has also been a surge of interest in recycling and experimenting with materials; knitting with rag, tape, string and other materials not previously considered.

Alongside knitting items for use or clothing is the development of the technique and process for its own sake, to make art forms; now knitting is no longer a craft that everyone can do, it can become something set apart. Some new knitting is wearable, such as jewellery knitted from wire and nylon filament: some pieces are installations or sculptures, using the technique to create structures where light may travel through and cast shadows, shapes can be built freely, and the technique enjoyed for its own sake.

Even into the electronic age, the opportunities that hand knitting has to offer 'ordinary' people (as well as 'artists') are relevant to our lives. There is a satisfaction in creating something by hand that is individual, with the possibility of making either clothing, or items for interiors, to co-ordinate with our present wardrobe or interior decoration. The technique of hand knitting gives freedom to move around, or to be creating in a small space, and not to be tied to equipment or machines. With a willingness to experiment and be imaginative, there are countless opportunities for creativity.

Peruvian finely knitted hat, and Andean doll with shaped legs and arms and knitted fingers and toes, and socks from around the world.

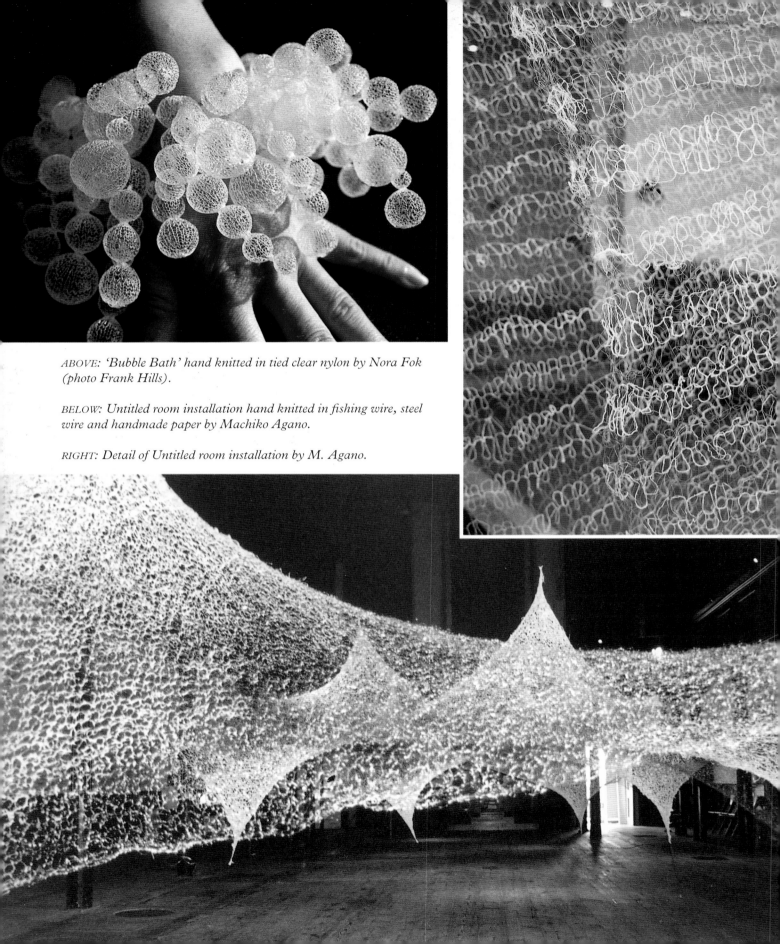

ABOVE: 'Bubble Bath' hand knitted in tied clear nylon by Nora Fok (photo Frank Hills).

BELOW: Untitled room installation hand knitted in fishing wire, steel wire and handmade paper by Machiko Agano.

RIGHT: Detail of Untitled room installation by M. Agano.

ABOVE: 'Drops of snow' hand-knitted choker in
silver wire by Tamami Uno.

RIGHT: Knitting with strips of silk and jersey
cotton.

3 HOW STITCHES WORK

HOW TO BEGIN

Edges: Casting On and Off

Edges in knitting are very important; they can spoil the whole effect if they are weak or wobbly, but give a professional decisive finish if done well and appropriately to the garment or knitted piece; rather like the way neat edges to flower borders can transform the look of the garden.

There are several ways of casting on stitches for knitting, each one giving a different kind of edge with different characteristics; some stretchy, some strong, some decorative; but they all involve making a chain of loops over the knitting needle which then become the first stitches to be worked into, and also form the first (usually bottom) edge. So the first decision depends on how this edge is going to be used: for instance the edge of a jumper needs to be stretchy in order to be pulled on over head, arms and shoulders, whereas on a jacket, waistcoat or cardigan, a firm non-stretchy edge would not be a problem. Some cast-on edges give a visual firm line of stitches at the bottom, and others can disappear into the knitting invisibly: others can be used to make a decorative or fancy edge. There are also ways of casting on to provide loops for picking up later and knitting in another direction rather than giving a finished edge. You may find you already have a way that is suitable for most purposes and use it all the time, but it is worth experimenting with some different methods to see their potential.

Casting off is less flexible than casting on: the loops are already on the needle, and have to be locked over each other sideways in order to prevent them running down and unravelling in a 'ladder'. The action of looping or locking one stitch over another immediately takes away its ability to stretch out: this is why a piece of crocheted fabric is less stretchy than knitting, because the structure is made by looping the stitches sideways over each other continuously, which gives it a firmer character in all directions.

The standard way of casting off leaves all stitches neatly joined in a chain along the top of the knitting, but has a tendency to be very firm, which can be a problem, for example particularly round necks. This edge looks like a crochet chain or row, which in fact is exactly what it is, and this way of casting off can be speeded up enormously by using a crochet hook instead of a needle in the right hand, and crocheting along the last row to give a finished edge by pulling the loops through with the hook rather than lifting over with the needle: one movement instead of two.

There are also a few ways of varying casting off to give a less visually hard line, and some different methods to make a more decorative edge.

The following methods are described with their uses, advantages and disadvantages, and instructions. There does not seem to be a universal name for the different methods, but as far as possible they are described with the most commonly used name, or by something that describes the process.

> **NOTE**
>
> In this book, the illustrated samples have been knitted in a plain, thick yarn in order to show the textures and stitches clearly. The effects will vary with other yarns.

OPPOSITE PAGE:
Samples of stitches, each worked with the same number of sts over the same number of rows, showing variations in width and length.

KNIT-ON CAST ON.

Hands casting on as left.

DESCRIPTION: often the first way learnt to cast on, this gives a rather loopy edge that can be corrected by knitting into the backs of the stitches on the first row, or alternatively the loops could be used for picking up later and knitting downwards, making a holey line through the fabric.
1) make a slip-loop onto LH needle
2) insert RH needle into loop and make a st
3) instead of slipping LH st off, put RH st onto LH needle, and rep from 2.

KNIT AND CAST OFF.
1) knit 2 sts
2) using the tip of the LH needle, lift the first st on RH needle over the last-knitted st. (i.e. RH st over LH st)
3) knit another st, and rep from 2.
   This is the most commonly used form of casting off, giving a neat chain edge with very little stretch. For a quicker method, use a crochet hook instead of the RH needle, and work single crochet to cast all the sts off.
   In this sample it is worked on the purl side.

SINGLE THUMB-TWIST CAST ON.
DESCRIPTION: this gives a fairly flexible edge, and is different from the knit-on and cable cast on, as the stitches are made on the RH needle, so is very useful if extra sts are needed in the middle of a row, for example, in buttonholes.
   It is difficult to knit the first row after this cast-on: *see* thumb twist with two ends.
1) make a slip loop on RH needle
2) twist yarn over L thumb by starting with the thumb above the yarn, and place on RH needle. Rep until you have enough sts.
   This sample has slipped sts at the edges: slip the first st of every row.

K-2-TOG CAST OFF.
DESCRIPTION: although the loops are still laid over each other, they go from left to right in pairs, instead of from right to left in a chain, so the appearance is different, and there is no visible hard line.
a) *K 2 tog, place RH st onto LH needle, and rep from *.

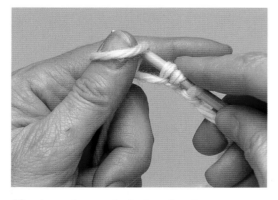

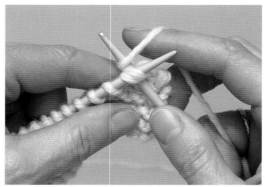

Hands casting on single thumb twist.   *Hands casting off K2 tog.*

2-END THUMB-TWIST CAST ON.

DESCRIPTION: this is the same as single thumb-twist cast on, but the first row is knitted as you go, making a firm but elastic edge. It produces a distinct knit and purl side.

Make a slip knot some way along the yarn, leaving a tail end that is used as in single thumb-twist cast on.

Insert the RH needle into the loop on the thumb and knit with the main yarn to make sts. This is, in effect, the same edge as single thumb twist. If the next row is treated as the right side, this cast on will show as a purl ridge. Alternatively, purl the first row, then have a smoother edge facing.

To calculate how long a tail to leave, try casting on, for instance, 20 sts, unravel, and measure how much 'tail' 20 sts needed. Multiply this up for the amount of sts you need.

VARIATION
Use a second colour instead of the 'tail' for a contrast edge.
This sample has the first st of every row worked (in knit or purl as appropriate).

Hands casting on 2-end thumb twist, yarn in RH.

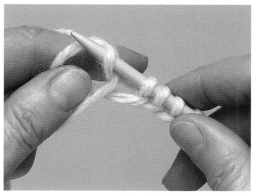

Hands casting on 2-end thumb twist, yarn in LH.

ABOVE RIGHT: *Hands casting on as above.*

CABLE CAST ON.

DESCRIPTION: this makes a good firm edge, without much stretch.
Begin as for knit-on cast on, but when 2 sts are made, * insert RH needle between the 2 sts, make a new st, and put back onto LH needle. Rep from *.

KNIT AND CAST OFF.

PICOT-POINT CAST ON.

Hands casting on as left.

DESCRIPTION: a decorative edge formed of a chain of little knots or 'blips', from which sts are picked up along the edge. If this is followed by a flat rather than gathered stitch, the edge shows more clearly: i.e. moss or garter st. It has often been used in lace knitting, and would work well with an open, lacy stitch.

2 sts are picked up from each 'point', so cast on half as many points as sts needed. If 1 st was picked up from each point, the effect would be more gathered and frilly.

To make the picot-point chain:
1) make a slip loop on LH needle
2) knit-on cast on to make 2 more sts
3) knit and cast off until 1 st left
4) put RH st back on LH needle, and rep from 2, until it is long enough.

TO PICK UP STS
Using the remaining stitch as the first stitch, work along the picot strip and pick up 2 loops from each 'point', so cast on half as many points as sts needed.

The sample has been knitted in chunky wool for clarity: knitted finely it makes a dainty edge.

K-2-TOG CAST OFF.

Diagram of picot-point cast-on.

INVISIBLE CAST ON FOR RIBBING OR DOUBLE-FABRIC (TUBULAR) KNITTING.

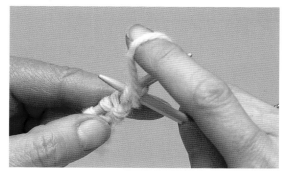

Hands casting on as left.

DESCRIPTION: a tidy, professional looking edge for ribbing, with no contrasting line: the sts grow from the very edge. It also makes a good edge when knitting a double fabric (*see* p.73).

Make a slip loop on LH needle, and cast on a 2nd st.
1) * insert RH needle from the back to the front bet these last 2 sts
2) take the yarn round the needle as if to purl, and draw the yarn thro onto the RH needle, taking care not to twist it as it is placed on LH needle
3) insert the RH needle from front to back bet the last 2 sts on LH needle
4) take the yarn round the needle as if to knit, and draw the yarn thro onto the RH needle, taking care not to twist it as it is placed on LH needle.

Cont from * until enough sts.
For ribbing: with an odd no of sts, begin the next row with a purl st: with an even no, begin with knit.
If using for double fabric knitting, K the K sts and slip the Ps.

CAST OFF IN RIB.

CAST-OFF CAST ON.
DESCRIPTION: this makes a firm chain edge, identical to chain cast-off, and uses a crochet hook to make the sts over the knitting needle. It could be used when cast on and off edges need to match: that is, if working a jacket across sideways from cuff to cuff, the cuffs would match, and so would front edges.
1) make a slip loop onto LH needle
2) holding yarn in left hand, use a crochet hook in RH, insert hook into loop and make a st, keeping it on the hook
3) place crochet hook over needle, and pick up yarn, pulling thro to make a st over the needle
4) pass yarn round so it is below needle again, and rep from 3.

The last st is transferred from the crochet hook to the needle.

KNIT AND CAST OFF.

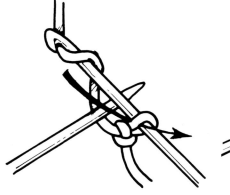

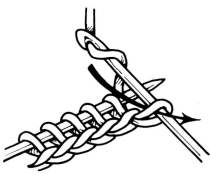

Hands casting on as above.   RIGHT: *Diagram of cast-off cast on.*

PROVISIONAL CAST ON.

DESCRIPTION: there are several methods of casting on which can be undone later to leave loops free for picking up and knitting downwards. There are lots of practical uses for this cast on: for example, on a garment the main body or sleeves could be knitted from this edge, then the welts picked up and knitted down, giving the opportunity to decide on welt design at the end. It also makes repairs easier on cuffs and edges to have them finishing in a cast-off edge.

The simplest way is to cast on as in 'cast-off cast on', using a contrast yarn, and instead of putting the last crochet loop on the needle, fasten it loosely and begin knitting in the main yarn. The cast on can then easily be unravelled later.

KNIT AND CAST OFF.

ABOVE AND RIGHT: Two stages of knotted edge cast on.

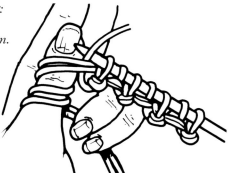

KNOTTED EDGE CAST ON, *Channel Island method.*

DESCRIPTION: this is a similar method to thumb twist with 2 ends, needing a tail of yarn (or second yarn) used double to make loops over the thumb, and a main yarn for making stitches. Alternate sts are knotted, with a plain 'yarn over needle' between each one. It produces a knotted edge, with the knots spaced out by the 'yarn overs': less pronounced knots than picot point, but firm, elastic and decorative.

It works best with thickish yarn to a fine needle: the effect is lost with loose tension, i.e. fine yarn to thicker needle.

Again, best used with a flat fabric: for instance, this cast on is used in the traditional Guernsey sweater, 5-ply wool is knitted on size 13 needles, followed by garter st.

Make a slip loop on RH needle, some way along the thread, as the tail end is used double.
1) twist the doubled end twice round the L thumb, beginning with the thumb under the yarn (in opposite direction to thumb-twist cast on), and knit thro both loops to make a st on RH needle with the single (main) yarn, pulling double yarn thro carefully until firm
2) place single yarn over RH needle (this makes a stitch).
Rep 1 and 2, so alternate sts have knots, with plain sts between.

PICOT-POINT CAST OFF.
DESCRIPTION: this is the same method of making little raised knots as picot-point cast on, but the knots can be spaced by a number of plain cast offs in between. Apart from being a decorative edge, it has much more stretch than a plain cast off, so works well for necks, cuffs and so on.
1) knit and cast off 3 sts
2) * put last RH st back on LH needle, and work as for picot-point cast on 2 and 3, then cast off 3 more normally, and rep from * (number of sts between can be varied).

STITCHES: BASIC LOOPS, KNIT AND PURL

The way 'knit' and 'purl' stitches are made was described in Chapter 1, but there are endless ways of combining these two stitches; both in order to make decorative textured patterns, and also in ways that can completely change the thickness, stretch and character of the knitted fabric.

Taking the best-known combination, stocking stitch; this has a smooth side showing the vertical sides of the knitted loop (the 'knit side), and a rough side where all the horizontal tops of the loop fall (the 'purl' side): these stitches are well represented on a knitting chart with a vertical line for knit, and horizontal for purl. Although the stocking-stitch fabric has a uniform plain smooth side and a plain rough side, it does not lie flat, but has a tendency to curl. On a rectangular piece of knitting, the side edges tend to curl knit-side-out, round towards the purl side, and the top and bottom edges do the opposite, curling towards the knit side, showing the purl stitches on top of the curl. This is of course why we usually use a different stitch that lies flat for welts and front bands of garments, to give firm, flat edges. However,

Stocking stitch fabric curls towards purl side at the sides and towards knit side at top and bottom.

the 'curl' has great design potential, and can be used in lots of ways. It is good to work with the nature of the fabric and the technique and use its characteristics to advantage rather than to fight against it.

Knitted fabric can be changed dramatically by combining knit and purl in different ways, and this is clearly illustrated by two examples, each with the same number of stitches and rows: ribbing and welting.

In ribbing, where the stitches are knitted in vertical columns of knit and purl (one + one, two + two, or wider), the purl stitches sink back and the knits come forward, so the fabric squeezes together widthways becom-

ing long and narrow, making a very elastic, firm stitch (not curling at the edges), which as we know well is ideal for edgings.

In welting, the arrangement of knits and purls is in horizontal bands of rows (again these can vary in width), and the opposite happens: the purl stitches push forward and the knits sink back, so the fabric pulls up lengthways becoming short and wide, although again is very elastic.

The tension created by placing knit and purl stitches next to each other, where one pushes forward and the other pulls back, is evident in moss stitch, where the stitches are placed alternately forming a flat, non-

RIBBING AND WELTING.

The same no of sts and rows can produce dramatically different sized pieces of knitting, caused by the way knit stitches behave next to purl stitches, either horizontally or vertically. These samples are knitted with the same number of stitches and same size needles.

Ribbing pulls in widthways: the knit sts come forward, and the purl sink back. This sample is K2, P2. > < [ ] ∨∧ –

Welting works in the opposite way: it pulls up lengthways, with the purl sts coming forward and knit sinking back. This sample is K2 rows, P2 rows.
∧ [ ] ∨∧ –

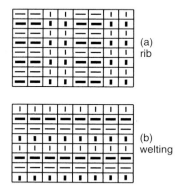

(a) rib

(b) welting

STITCHES AND CHARTS USED IN TRADITIONAL FISHERMEN'S SWEATERS.

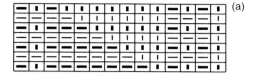 (a)

fishermen's patterns

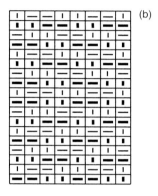 (b)

curling textured fabric which tends to be wider and shorter than stocking stitch. Moss stitch is usually knit one, purl one: if the knits and purls are used alternating in larger groups, textured patterns can be made with purls coming forward horizontally, and sinking back vertically.

There are some good examples of decorative patterns using knit and purl in the traditional fishermen's ganseys made around the coasts of Britain, often using a stocking-stitch background, with purl stitches placed individually or in pairs in vertical, diagonal and horizontal patterns which show beautifully in the smooth, strong yarns and firm

tensions used. Often the lower part of the garments were plain (that is, stocking stitch), and the more textured and patterned yokes made a thicker, warmer fabric over the chest and shoulders.

Another interesting example of patterns produced by knit and purl alone can be seen in a piece of fine Dutch knitting of the nineteenth century at the Victoria and Albert Museum, London. Here the scale of the design is large, made possible by the closeness of the tension, and birds and foliage are represented in combinations of purl, moss stitch and double moss stitch on a knit ground.

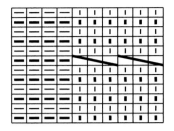

VERTICAL CABLES
>< [ ].
In this sample, the cables are worked on groups of 6 sts in stocking st, against a reverse stocking st (purl side) background.
Right-side rows: K6, P4, repeat as many times as you want.
Wrong side rows: K4, P6, repeating as before to make a wide rib.
Cont this rib for 5 rows, then every 6th row work the cables:
*slip 3 sts onto a cable (or spare double-ended) needle, and hold at the front. K3, then knit the 3 sts from the cable needle; P4. Repeat from *, but you can change the twist of the cable from right-over-left to left-over-right by holding the cable needle to the back of the work.

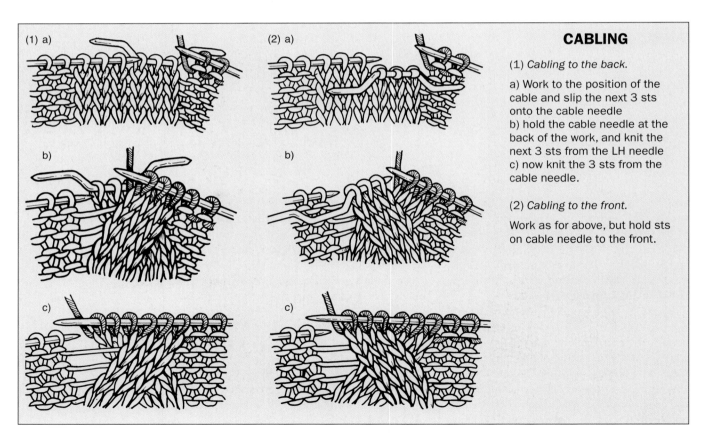

CABLING

(1) *Cabling to the back.*

a) Work to the position of the cable and slip the next 3 sts onto the cable needle
b) hold the cable needle at the back of the work, and knit the next 3 sts from the LH needle
c) now knit the 3 sts from the cable needle.

(2) *Cabling to the front.*

Work as for above, but hold sts on cable needle to the front.

CROSS-OVER STITCHES AND CABLES

Crossing one stitch over another makes a very distinct mark on the fabric, and has great possibilities for design. Stitches can be crossed over individually, in pairs, or greater numbers. If only one stitch is being crossed over one other, it is possible to knit by working into the second stitch on the needle and then the first, and lifting both off together. If two or more stitches are being moved, a 'cable' needle is useful: this is a short needle, pointed at both ends that hangs behind or in front of the work while the next stitches are worked, then the stitches on the cable needle are pulled across and knitted. It helps if the cable needle is shaped with a dip in the middle, as the stitches are less likely to slide off.

Because stitches are built in vertical columns, this kind of stitching lends itself to making vertical stripes, with the cross-overs falling above each other as in cables.

By following the direction of the crossed-over stitch, it is also easy to build patterns with a diagonal emphasis. If stitches or groups of stitches travel in both directions diagonally, trellis patterns are formed.

Although patterns in cabling or cross-over are usually regular and geometric (it is easier to knit regular patterns), they can also be used in a free way, letting the stitches twist and travel organically across the fabric.

We usually see crossed-over stitches and cables worked in knit stitches on a purl (or reverse stocking-stitch) background, because they show up most clearly in this way: therefore, the reverse can be utilized, and more subtle patterns made by avoiding this combination, perhaps working all

TRELLIS >< [ ] –.
In this sample, single sts are crossed over one st every right-side row, so that they travel smoothly in diagonal lines, crossing each other to make a trellis.
Cast on a multiple of 6 sts.
Row 1) (right side) * K1, P4, K1*, rep to end
Row 2) * P1, K1, P1 * rep to end
Row 3) *P 2nd st on needle, then K 1st st, and slip both off together. P 2, K 2nd st, P 1st st, and slip both off. *Alternatively, use a cable needle, or just slip the st off and hang on to it while you work the next st. The knit sts always cross in front of the purls.
Row 4) * K1, P1, K2, P1, K1* rep
Row 5) * P1, P 2nd st on needle, then K 1st st, and slip both off, K 2nd st, P 1st st, and slip both off, P1*
Row 6) * K2, P2, K2 * rep
Row 7) * P2, K 2nd st, K 1st st, slip both off, P2* rep

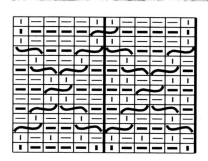

Row 8) * K2, P2, K2 * rep
Row 9) * P1, K 2nd st, P 1st st, slip both off, P 2nd st on needle, then K 1st , slip both off, P1 * rep
Row 10) as row 4
Row 11) * K 2nd st, P 1st st, slip both off, P2, P 2nd st on needle, then K 1st , slip both off, * rep
Row 12) * P1, K4, P1 * rep
Row 13) K1 * P4, K 2nd st, K 1st st, slip both off (crossing them the other way),* rep to end, K1
Row 14) as row 12.
Begin again from row 3.

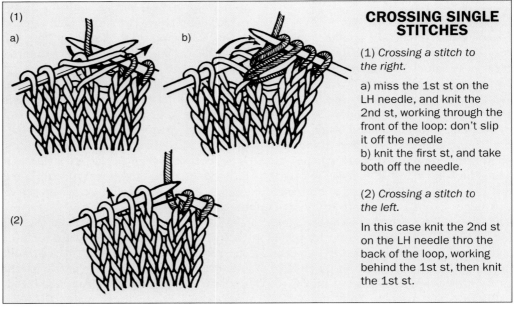

CROSSING SINGLE STITCHES

(1) *Crossing a stitch to the right.*

a) miss the 1st st on the LH needle, and knit the 2nd st, working through the front of the loop: don't slip it off the needle
b) knit the first st, and take both off the needle.

(2) *Crossing a stitch to the left.*

In this case knit the 2nd st on the LH needle thro the back of the loop, working behind the 1st st, then knit the 1st st.

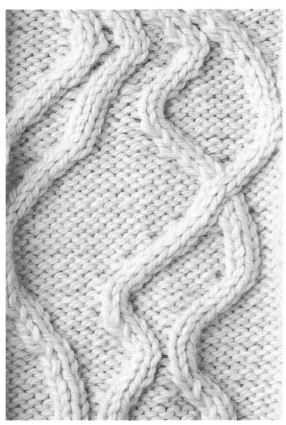

ABOVE: *SMOOTH RANDOM CABLES > < [ ].*
Both the travelling sts and the background are knit-face stocking-stitch.

LEFT: *RANDOM CABLES > < [ ].*
Groups of 2 knit sts travelling across a purl stocking-stitch background.

'BASKET WEAVE' CABLE > < [ ]
– |.

2 sts cross over the neighbouring 2 sts on alt
rows, making a very thick, firm fabric, that
pulls in substantially compared with stocking
stitch.
Multiple of 4 sts.
The cable movement is described: C4 front
or back:
Slip next 2 sts onto a cable needle and hold
at front or back of work, knit next 2 sts from
LH needle, then knit sts from cable needle.
Work 2 or more foundation rows in stocking
st.
Row 1) * C4 front, rep all along row from *
Row 2) purl
Row 3) K2 * C4 back, rep from * to last 2 sts,
K2
Row 4) purl
Rep these 4 rows.

in knit-face stocking stitch. It is worth
experimenting (*see* p.50, right).

The most important structural characteristic of cross-over knitting or cable patterns
is that because stitches are pulled across
each other, some of the stretch of the fabric
is lost, and it becomes narrower and tighter
widthways. Occasional cables do not make
very much difference to the stretchiness,
but an all-over pattern in cabling, for
instance a trellis pattern, will be very firm
and thick. It is the extra thickness of the
fabric produced that makes these stitches so
successful for warm clothing (*see* Trellis,
p.49 and 'Basket weave' Cable, above).

SLIP STITCHES

Here is a huge range of stitches, useful for
decorative patterns using colour and texture, and for creating thicker fabrics, that
are very easy and unfiddly to work. The
principle is to slip certain stitches in each
row without knitting them, from the left to
the right needle, leaving the knitting yarn to
strand across behind or in front of the
stitches slipped. If the yarn is stranded on
the back of the fabric, the slipped stitch
becomes a vertical decorative element: if it is
stranded at the front, there is a horizontal
decorative 'bar'. Stitches may be slipped for
one row, two rows or more, and in the
process, the fabric is pulled up lengthways.
Depending on the amount of stitches
slipped in each row, and the number of rows
they are slipped, the knitting can grow
rather slowly as only some of the stitches are
being worked each time, and the result is a
thick, textured or patterned fabric.

In this section we are looking at patterns
made by stitches alone, but slip stitches
have enormous potential for colour knitting (*see* Chapter 4).

Slip stitches can be worked in stocking
stitch, or in combinations of knit and purl
for extra texture and, as well as making
small repeated patterns, can also be used
for large-scale designs.

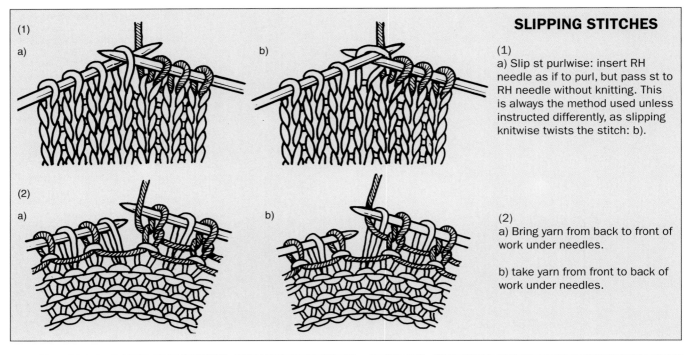

SLIPPING STITCHES

(1)
a) Slip st purlwise: insert RH needle as if to purl, but pass st to RH needle without knitting. This is always the method used unless instructed differently, as slipping knitwise twists the stitch: b).

(2)
a) Bring yarn from back to front of work under needles.

b) take yarn from front to back of work under needles.

SLIP ST TWEED > < ^ – |.
This produces a smooth fabric that has several characteristics of woven fabric, both in appearance, and in the smooth, flat (non-curling) drape, and lack of stretch.
Cast on an uneven no of sts.
Row 1) (right side) K1 * yf, S1 purlwise, yb, K1. Rep from * to end
Row 2) P2 * yb, S1 purlwise, yf, P1. Rep from * to last st, P1.
Rep these 2 rows.

ABOVE: Back of Slip st tweed.

HONEYCOMB SLIP ST.

Multiple of 8 sts + 4 edge sts.
Row 1) knit
Row 2) knit
Row 3) K1, S2 * K6, S2, rep from * to last st, K1
Row 4) P1, S2 * P6, S2, rep from * to last st, P1
Row 5) as row 3
Row 6) as row 4
Row 7) as row 3
Row 8) as row 4
Row 9) knit
Row 10) knit
Row 11) K5, S2 * K6, S2, rep from * ending K5
Row 12) P5, S2 * P6, S2, rep from * ending P5
Row 13) as row 11
Row 14) as row 12
Row 15) as row 11
Row 16) as row 12
Rep from row 3.

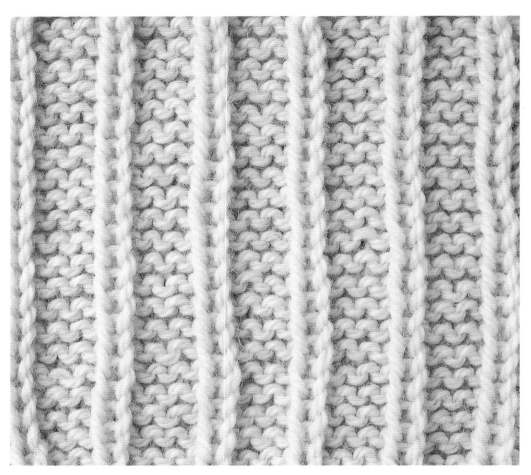

SLIP ST TEXTURED STRIPES [ ].

Cast on a multiple of 5 sts.
Row 1) wrong side: K2 * P1, K4, rep from * ending P1, K2
Row 2) K2 * S1 purlwise, K4, rep from * ending S1 purlwise, K2.
The combination of garter and slip st makes quite a thick fabric that is very different on each side.

LEFT: *Back of slip st textured stripes.*

INCREASING AND DECREASING

Stitches can be increased or decreased to change the width of the fabric at the edges, or within the fabric.

Shaping at the edges allows the rest of the knitting to lie flat with the pattern uninterrupted. It can be carried out right on the edge stitch, or two or three stitches away, making a more decorative edge.

Increasing

There are several ways of increasing, each making a different mark in the knitting, so experiment to see which seems suitable for your design.

◆ Yarn over: place the yarn over the needle between stitches, and knit (or purl) this loop in the following row, making an extra stitch.

Result: a hole is made where the yarn went over

a) knit row

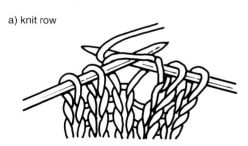

b) purl row

Yarn over.

◆ Pick up yarn between the stitches, knit or purl it to make an extra stitch.

Result: this makes a smaller hole than yarn over, and can be twisted to close the hole.

a) M1 (pick up bar)

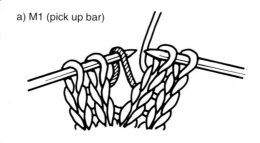

b) twist bar to close hole

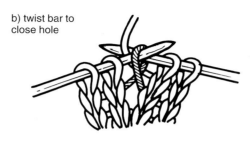

Pick up yarn between the stitches.

◆ Pick up the loop of the stitch below, and knit or purl it.

Result: a smoother, less noticeable increase.

Pick up the loop of the stitch below.

These increases can be made at the beginning or end of the row, or 2 sts from the edge, as shown.

◆ Knit (or purl) into the front and back of next stitch to make two stitches.

Result: the increased stitch produces a little bar on the second stitch, which needs to be placed appropriately to the pattern being used.

Knit (or purl) into the front and back of st.

Decreasing

Turning two stitches into one can be done by crossing: a) right over left, or b) left over right:

a) There are two well-known ways of doing this:

   i) Knit 1, slip 1 knitwise, pass slip stitch over (K1, S1, psso).
   ii) Slip next 2 sts knitwise, put them back on the LH needle the other way around and knit through both tog (SSK).

These both make right cross over left.

Structurally, these two methods perform the same task, but you may find that the first method stretches the top (slipped) stitch slightly, and that the second method, more commonly used in the USA, is neater.

b) Knit 2 together (K2 tog) crosses left over right.

These can be formed in purl or knit.

Increases and decreases can be used in conjunction, perhaps alternately along the row, to make a fabric where the number of stitches remains constant, but the direction of the stitches is tilted by these movements so that the fabric waves or zig-zags between shapings. This not only has lots of scope for decorative patterning, but also affects the hang or drape of the fabric. If the stitches are travelling in a diagonal direction instead of vertically or horizontally, it behaves rather like a woven fabric when used on the bias, and drapes beautifully.

Again, there are opportunities for combining these stitches with colour, as covered in Chapter 4.

Shaping within the fabric may call for a 'double' increase or decrease, making or losing two stitches instead of one.

Increasing

Any of the increases above can be used on either side of a central stitch for a symmetrical double increase.

◆ yarn over can be either side of a central stitch

◆ picking up the strand can be either side of a central stitch

◆ picking up the loop from the stitch below would be difficult to do on either side of a central stitch, so could be combined with one of the other increases to make a pair

◆ knitting into the front and back of 2 consecutive stitches, the second stitch becomes central to the increases.

Multiple increases can be made by knitting alternately into the front and back of the same stitches to create from three to seven stitches (*see* Embossed Knitting, p.63).

ZIG-ZAG TEXTURES

^ [ ] / ⌄ −.

Cast on a multiple of 9 sts.
Row 1) * K2 tog, K1, K into F and B of next st,
K into F and B of next st, K2, S1, K1, psso.
Rep from *
Row 2) purl
Row 3) as row 1
Row 4) knit
Row 5) purl
Row 6) knit
Rep these 6 rows.

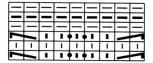

Decreasing

Decreases can either be paired next to each other, or either side of a centre stitch, or three stitches can be decreased straight into one.

Either: Slip 2 knitwise, Knit 1, pass both slipped sts over (S2, K1, p2sso).

This makes a strong vertical central stitch with decreases fitting neatly either side

or: Slip 1, Knit 2 together, pass slip stitch over (S1, K2 tog, psso): here the 3 sts cluster together.

These increases and decreases all have quite different visual results

EYELETS AND LACE

Learning to make holes in knitting gives another design tool. Holes can be placed in any arrangement, as individual units, in geometric patterns, or freely and randomly. We have looked at traditional lace knitting from the Shetland Islands using fine wool, and at fine cotton lace knitting in mats and bedspreads. These sorts of stitches can also be used in contemporary clothing or pieces for interiors. Holed knitting does not have to be fine and lacy, it can also be carried out in thick yarns, in linen or string, or in chunky wool.

The principle of making holes is to place the yarn over the needle between stitches, and knit (or purl) this loop in the following row, leaving a hole where the yarn went over ('O') (*see* p.55). If you

SHAPING AT THE EDGE

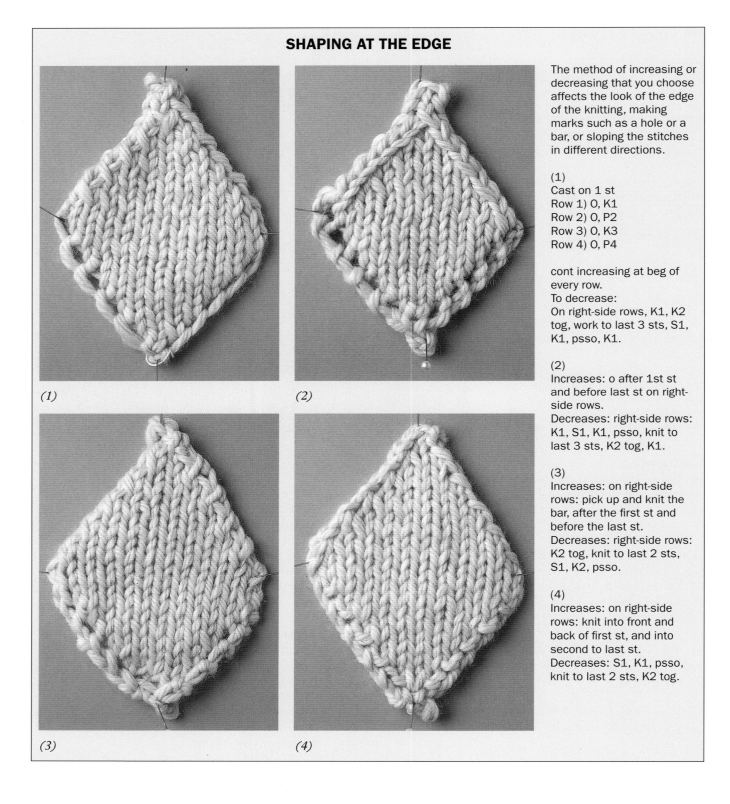

(1)

(2)

(3)

(4)

The method of increasing or decreasing that you choose affects the look of the edge of the knitting, making marks such as a hole or a bar, or sloping the stitches in different directions.

(1)
Cast on 1 st
Row 1) O, K1
Row 2) O, P2
Row 3) O, K3
Row 4) O, P4

cont increasing at beg of every row.
To decrease:
On right-side rows, K1, K2 tog, work to last 3 sts, S1, K1, psso, K1.

(2)
Increases: o after 1st st and before last st on right-side rows.
Decreases: right-side rows: K1, S1, K1, psso, knit to last 3 sts, K2 tog, K1.

(3)
Increases: on right-side rows: pick up and knit the bar, after the first st and before the last st.
Decreases: right-side rows: K2 tog, knit to last 2 sts, S1, K2, psso.

(4)
Increases: on right-side rows: knit into front and back of first st, and into second to last st.
Decreases: S1, K1, psso, knit to last 2 sts, K2 tog.

SHAPING WITHIN THE KNITTED FABRIC

(1)

(2)

(3)

(4)

This is used in bias fabrics and lace stitches, and tilts groups of stitches so that areas of the fabric slope in different directions.

All increases and decreases in the following pieces are worked on right-side rows.

(1) Increases: mark a centre st, and increase either side of it.
Work to centre, O, K1, O, work to end.
Decreases: work to 2 sts before centre, S1, K1, psso, K1, K2 tog.

(2) Increases: mark centre st, and pick up bar and K either side of centre st.
Decreases: work to 1 st before centre, Sl, K2 tog, psso.

(3) Increases: mark centre st, work to centre, pick up loop from centre st in row below, K centre st, pick up same loop and knit again.
Decreases: work to 1 st before centre, S2, K1, p2sso (pass 2 slip sts over).

(4) Increases: work to 1 st before centre, K into F and B, K into F and B of centre st, work to end.
Decreases: work to 2 sts before centre, K2 tog, K centre st, S1, K1, psso, work to end.

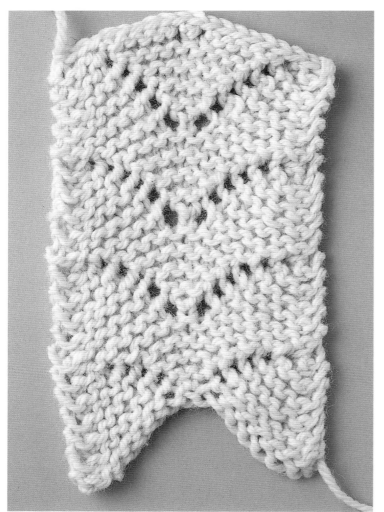

SHETLAND LEAF O / ∧ –.
This is a garter stitch lacy strip, that could be used as a border.
Cast on 19 sts.
Row 1) K1, K2 tog, K6, O, K1, O, K6, K2 tog, K1
Row 2) and alternate rows, knit
Row 3) K1, K2 tog, K5, O, K3, O, K5, K2 tog, K1
Row 5) K1, K2 tog, K4, O, K5, O, K4, K2 tog, K1
Row 7) K1, K2 tog, K3, O, K7, O, K3, K2 tog, K1
Row 9) K1, K2 tog, K2, O, K9, O, K2, K2 tog, K1
Row 11) K1, K2 tog, K1, O, K5, O, K1, O, K5, O, K1, K2 tog, K1
Row 12) K1, K2 tog, K to last 3 sts, K2 tog, K1.
Rep from row 3.
NB there are 19 sts in every row except row 11.

want your number of stitches to stay even, there needs to be a decreased stitch to balance the 'yarn over', or an extra stitch will result. As the decrease is also decorative, and can be made by stitches crossing left over right or right over left (by K2 tog, or K1, S1, psso, *see* p.55), this will make a great difference to the look of the fabric.

If the decrease is kept next to the 'yarn over', it makes a flat lacy pattern.

If the decrease is some distance away from the 'yarn over', all the stitches will move away from the increase towards the decrease, which can give an undulating movement to the pattern (*see* 'Different Directions', p.65, for more on bias fabrics).

LACY LEAF PATTERN O / ⌣ –.

23 sts.
Row 1) * O, K1, O, K2 (K2 tog) × 2, K2; rep from * once (O, K2 tog) × 2, K1
Row 2) and all even rows, purl
Row 3) O, K3, O, K1 (K2 tog) × 2, K1. Rep from * once, (O, K2 tog) × 2, K1
Row 5) * O, K5, O, (K2 tog) × 2, Rep from * once, (O, K2 tog) × 2, K1
Row 7) * O, K3, K2 tog, K2, O, K2 tog, Rep from * once, (O, K2 tog) × 2, K1
Row 8) purl.

REPEATING LEAVES O / ⌄.

Rep of 16 sts, + 3 edge sts.
1) * P3, K9, P3, K1 * rep, end P3
2) * K3, P1, K3, P9 * end K3
3) * P3, K3, S2, K1, p2sso, K3, P3, M1, K1, M1, * rep, end P3
4) * K3, P3, K3, P7, * end K3
5) * P3, K2, S2, K1, p2sso, K2, P3, K1, M1, K1, M1, K1,* rep, end P3
6) * K3, P5 * rep, end K3
7) * P3, K1, S2, K1, p2sso, K1, P3, K2, M1, K1, M1, K2, * end P3
8) * K3, P7, K3, P3* end K3
9) * P3, S2, K1, p2sso, P3, K3, M1, K1, M1, K3, * end P3
10) * K3, P9, K3, P1, * end K3
11) * P3, M1, K1, M1, P3, K3, S2, K1, p2sso, K3 * end P3
12) as row 8
13) * P3, K1, M1, K1, M1, K1, P3, K2, S2, K1, p2sso, K2, * end P3
14) as row 6
15) *P3, K2, M1, K1, M1, K2, P3, K1, S2, K1, p2sso, K1,* end P3
16) as row 4
17)* P3, K3, M1, K1, M1, K3, P3, S2, K1, p2sso,* end P3
18) as row 2.
Begin again from row 3.

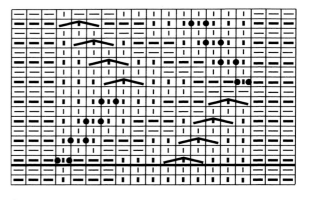

EMBOSSED KNITTING

Increases and decreases can be used to shape small areas of the knitting into individual motifs that grow or bulge from the surface. Beginning with one stitch, and increasing on either side for a few rows, then decreasing again, 'leaf' and 'bell' shapes can be made. Like cables, these stand out well from a purl background.

Shapes can also begin with a multiple increase, for instance making five stitches from one (knit into the front, back, front, back, and front again, then take all sts off the needle), working on these five stitches for a few rows, then decreasing them just as rapidly by passing all the extra stitches over the original one stitch, to produce a 'bobble'.

BOBBLES [ ].

Bobbles can be small, that is, 3 sts, or large, perhaps 7 sts. They can increase to full size over 3 rows by increasing a few stitches at a time, and decrease in the same way, or increase and decrease immediately as described above. They can also be made knit or purl side out: once again, experimenting is useful.

SHORT ROWS

Another way of giving a third dimension to the flat surface of the knitted fabric by making small areas of the fabric distort or bulge is to knit 'short rows'. Where 'embossed knitting' makes vertical bulges, short rows work horizontally. An example of this effect used in a traditional way,

There are plenty of different ways of making bobbles: here are 3, all worked on a purl stocking-stitch background.
a) purl side out (left of sample)
K into front, back and front of next st to make 3 sts, turn, K3, turn, P3, turn, K3, turn, P3 tog
b) larger (centre)
make 5 sts by knitting into front, back, front, back and front of st, turn. K5, turn, P5, turn, K5, turn, P5, turn, pass 2nd, 3rd, 4th and 5th sts over the 1st st
c) knit side out (right of sample).
Work to position of bobble, right-side facing.
K into front, back and front of next st to make 3 sts, turn, purl back.
Turn, K3, turn, P3, turn, K3 tog.

SHORT ROW WAVY TEXTURES [ ] ⌒.

Worked on 27 sts, this uses short rows to distort the fabric.
K2 foundation rows.
Row 1)* K9, turn: S1, P7, turn: S1, K6, turn: S1, P5, turn: S1, K4, turn: S1, P3, turn: S1, K3, turn: S1, P4, turn:
S1, K5, turn: S1, P6, turn: S1, K7, turn: S1, P8, turn, K9 *
Rep * to * all along the row for each group of 9 sts
Row 2) knit
Row 3) purl
Row 4) knit
Row 5) K5, turn: S1, P4, turn: K4, turn: S1, P3, turn: K3, turn: S1, P2, turn: K4, turn: S1, P3, turn: K5.
Work as row 1 * to * to last 4 sts:
K4 turn: P4, turn: S1, K3, turn: P3, turn: S1, K2, turn: P3, turn: S1, K2, turn: P4, turn: S1, K3
Row 6) knit
Row 7) purl
Row 8) knit
Rep these 8 rows.

where the purpose is functional rather than decorative, is a sock heel. The stitches for the heel area are worked backwards and forwards on their own, in shorter and shorter then longer and longer rows, until the three-dimensional heel shape bulges out (*see* p.81).

To try this idea in a piece of knitting, knit to the end of your chosen group of stitches and, without finishing the row, turn and purl back over these few stitches. Turn again, and knit another shorter row, perhaps one or two stitches less, and turn again. Work a shorter row each time until only two or three stitches are left (or even right down to one stitch, which will produce a pointed shape), then carry on working back and forth over these stitches, working two or three more every row until all are joined in again.

These 'bulges' can be worked as motifs, or made into all-over patterns (*see* p.64).

Other ways of using short rows could be to make flaps coming out of, and perhaps joining into the fabric again: either as decoration, or in a functional way, for example a pocket lining.

DIFFERENT DIRECTIONS

Leading on from the previous section, an example of a stitch that uses short rows all over is the 'entrelac' or 'basket weave'

BASIC ENTRELAC, 6-ST REPEAT
< > /.

In these instructions, the main building blocks are printed bold, all triangles (bottom edge, sides and top edge) are in plain print.

Cast on a multiple of 6 sts (18 sts would be enough for a first sample)
Base triangles: *P2 (this is wrong side facing), turn and K2, turn and P3, turn and K3, turn and P4, turn and K4, turn and P5, turn and K5, turn and P6. Leave these sts, and repeat from * on the next group of 6. Work again, making 3 base triangles.

1ST ROW OF RECTANGLES (INCLUDING SIDE TRIANGLES)
NB colour can be changed for each row or block.

SIDE TRIANGLE
K2, turn and P2, turn; inc in 1st st (by knitting into front and back of st), S1, K1 (this is 1st st of next group), psso; turn and P3; turn, inc in 1st st, K1, S1, K1, psso; turn and P4; turn, inc in first st, K2, S1, K1 psso; turn and P5; turn, inc in 1st st, K3, S1, K1, psso. Edge triangle complete.

KNIT BLOCKS
* Pick up and K6 sts evenly along edge of next triangle (turn and P6, turn and K5, S1, K1, psso) 6 times = 1 block complete. Rep from * to edge of last triangle.

LAST SIDE TRIANGLE
Pick up and K6 evenly along edge of last base triangle, turn and P2 tog, P4; turn and K5; turn and P2 tog, P3; turn and K4; turn and P2 tog, P2; turn and K3; turn and P2 tog, P1; turn and K2; turn and P2 tog. 1 st remains on RH needle, and edge triangle is complete.

PURL BLOCKS
Using st on RH needle, pick up and P5 sts evenly along edge of triangle just finished. (Turn and K6, turn and P5, P2 tog) 6 times, then cont as follows:
* Pick up and P6 sts evenly along side of next block (turn and K6, turn and P5, P2 tog) 6 times, rep from * to end.

stitch. Here a row of blocks is built up, each knitted backwards and forwards individually, which interlinks with the neighbouring blocks as it goes, making a fabric composed of blocks or rectangles where the stitches all travel diagonally, or in a bias direction.

These can be any size, colour, or be knitted in different stitches, in patterns or in a random effect, opening up exciting design opportunities. The effort of constantly turning the work is greater if the number of stitches of each block is small, for example perhaps only four, six or eight stitches, and it may be worth trying Elizabeth

Knit blocks are now worked as before, but picking up from edges of purl blocks. Alternate the knit and purl blocks, with side triangles if necessary, finishing with knit blocks, then work:

TOP TRIANGLES
Using st left on RH needle, pick up and P5 sts evenly along edge of block or triangle just worked. Turn and K6; turn and P2 tog, P3, P2 tog; turn and K5; turn and P2 tog, P2, P2 tog; turn and K4; turn and P2 tog, P1, P2 tog; turn and K3; turn and P2 tog twice; turn and K2; turn and P1, P2 tog, P1; turn and K3; turn and P3 tog; rep from *, as many times as needed.

The sample illustrated is knitted in stocking st with one row of reverse stocking st through the centre of each block. There are endless design opportunities with entrelac stitch, using colours, different textured stitches, or a combination of both.

Entrelac.

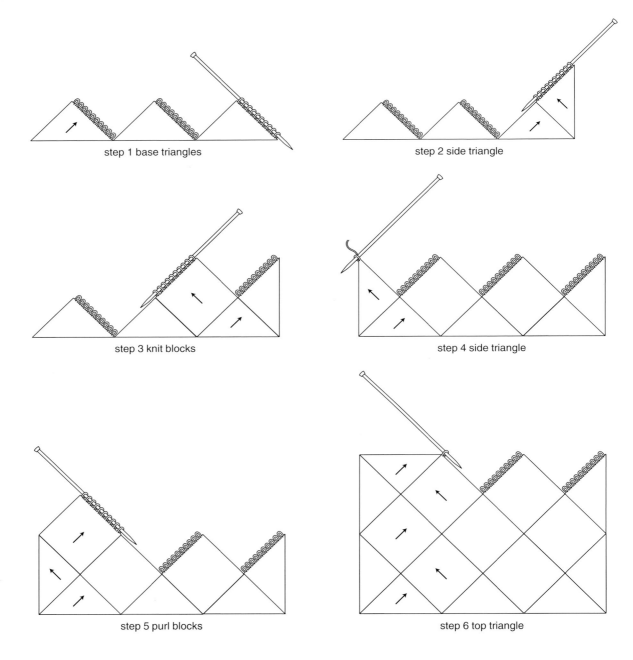

step 1 base triangles

step 2 side triangle

step 3 knit blocks

step 4 side triangle

step 5 purl blocks

step 6 top triangle

Zimmerman's idea (*see* Chapter 1, 'Knitting Technique') of 'knitting back backwards': that is, if working in stocking stitch, instead of turning at the end of each group of stitches to purl back, knit in mirror image, from the right-hand needle to the left, in 'reverse knit'. In this way, stocking stitch is made by working alternately off one needle, then the other, without turning.

Knitting a sample or square piece in entrelac is much more complicated than knitting a larger piece in the round, as you have to learn to make triangles for the straight edges. If you knit a larger piece in the round, it fits together seamlessly, using only the building blocks, with no edges necessary. However, it is useful to know how to make side and top triangles as well, as they will be needed occasionally to shape garments or other items.

Entrelac is an example of organized or formalized directional knitting, with stitches picked up along the sides of each block and knitted at right angles to it. This technique can be used with any knitting: stitches can be picked up round an arm-hole and sleeves knitted downwards, stitches can be picked up along the bottom edge of a garment or bedspread, and a border knitted on. With a cushion, stitches may be picked up all round the edge to knit a border 'in the round', perhaps making it square by increasing at each corner.

Taking this idea further, random shapes could be made by picking up stitches, knitting one piece on from another in a free way. However, to achieve a completely free and organic look is more difficult than it might seem, as the stitches used will influence how flat the shapes will lie. It needs to look as if it was meant to be, and was not a complete surprise to the knitter: this needs some skill, so probably some sampling and experimenting will help.

Some different ways of using entrelac stitch.

SOME DIFFERENT DIRECTIONS IN KNITTING TO TRY

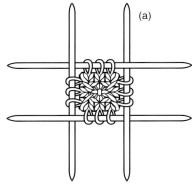

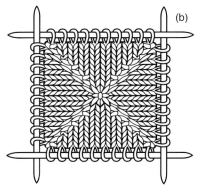

ABOVE LEFT: SQUARE
KNITTED FROM CENTRE.
Cast on 4 sts. Using a set of 5 double-ended needles, begin knitting in the round:
Round 1) O, knit into front and back of st, onto each of 4 needles
Round 2) knit
Round 3) O, K2, knit into front and back of st, onto each of 4 needles
Round 4) knit
Round 5) O, K4, knit into front and back of st, onto each of 4 needles
Round 6) knit.
Cont increasing in this way, at beg and end of each needle, until you reach the size you want.

SQUARE WITH EXTRA CORNERS.
Work as for above, then work corners individually.
On this sample the corners are worked in contrast colour for clarity.
Working one corner at a time, decrease at either end of every right-side row, until all sts are gone.

*ABOVE: a) Beginning square
knitted from centre.*
*b) Stage 2 of square knitted
from centre.*

SQUARE WITH BORDER.

A small central square has been knitted, and then the stitches picked up along all 4 sides, and a border knitted outwards.

Use circular needles if enough sts, otherwise double-ended needles, one for each side of the square, knitting with a 5th.

Increase at every corner: imagining that each side of the square is a 'row', knit into the front and back of 1st st, then knit to last st before corner, knit into front and back of last st.

Increase on alternate rounds.

BELOW: *(a) Beginning of square with border.*
(b) Stage 2 of square with border.

(a)

(b)

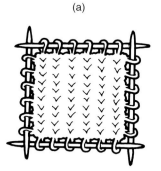

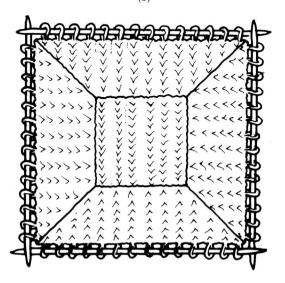

DIAGONAL SQUARE.

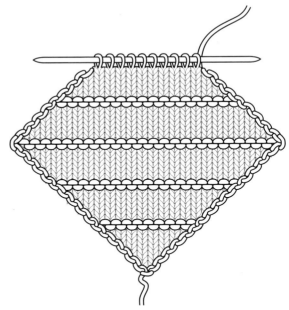

Method of knitting diagonal square.

Cast on 1 st. Increase 1 st at beg of every row, working in pattern:
Row 1) knit
Row 2) purl
Row 3) knit
Row 4) knit.
When there are enough sts for the diagonal, cast off 1 st at beg of each row.

SPIRAL SQUARE.

Cast on 4 sts. Using a set of 5 double-ended needles, begin knitting in the round:
Round 1) col A: O, K1 onto each of 4 needles
Round 2) col A: O, P2 onto each of 4 needles
Round 3) col B: O, K3 onto each of 4 needles
Round 4) col B: O, K4 onto each of 4 needles.
Rep these stripes, increasing before the first st on each needle, until the size you want.

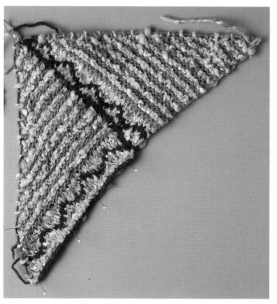

SQUARE MADE WITH 4 DIAGONAL TRIANGLES: 2 SHOWN.

1ST TRIANGLE: cast on sts for the base, which will form half the diagonal of the square.

This right-angle triangle is formed by decreasing at the edge that will be the outside of the square.

Knitting every row (in this sample, 2 rows each colour), decrease 1 st at the end of every right-side row, and continue until all sts are used up.

NEXT TRIANGLE: pick up the same no of sts that you cast on for 1st triangle, along the right-hand (right-angle) edge, and make 2nd triangle. Make 3rd and 4th in same way, leaving one seam to be sewn at the end.

VARIATIONS
This shaping works in garter st, but other sts will necessitate different amounts of decreases: for instance, in stocking st this would be a much longer, thinner triangle, and you would need to decrease sts more rapidly to make the ¼ square proportion, perhaps every row.
Instead of decreasing, the sts could be left on a thread for the outside edges of the square. These sts could then be picked up to knit a border, but extra sts would have to be added, as this edge is longer than the cast-on edge.

(a)

(b)

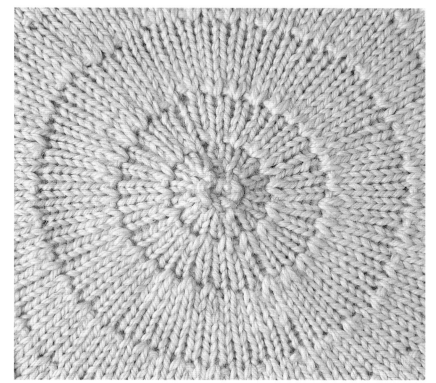

MARY THOMAS'S CIRCULAR 'MEDALLION'.

This is a circle knitted from the centre outwards, with increases evenly spread throughout, taken from Mary Thomas's book of knitting patterns of 1943.
Cast on 8 sts, arranging 2 on each of 4 double-ended needles, and knitting with the 5th.
Round 1) knit into back of all sts
Round 2) M1 into every st
Rounds 3, 4, 5) knit
Round 6) M1 into every st
Rounds 7–11) knit
Round 12) M1 into every st
Rounds 13–19) knit
Round 20) M1 into every 2nd st
Rounds 21–25) knit
Round 26) M1 into every 3rd st
Rounds 27 – 31) knit
Round 32) M1 into every 4th st.
Cont in this way knitting 5 rounds plain then an inc round, the next being M1 into every 5th st, and so on.

SPIRAL CIRCLE (OR HEXAGON), 6 INCS.

Using 4 double-ended needles, cast 6 sts onto 1 needle.
Round 1) knit the sts onto 3 needles, with 'O, K1, O, K1' on each needle
Round 2) knit
Round 3) O, K2, O, K2 on each needle
Round 4) knit
Round 5) O, K3, O, K3 on each needle
Round 6) knit.
Cont in this way, increasing at the beginning and middle of each needle.

VARIATIONS

'O' leaves a hole that can be decorative: use a different increase if you don't want a hole.

This circle will not lie flat in stocking st, as there are not enough increases. As it is slightly domed, it makes a good shape for a hat top.

If garter st is used, or alternate stripes of garter and stocking st, the circle will lie flatter.
Cast off loosely.

SPIRAL CIRCLE (OR OCTAGON), 8 INCS.

Worked exactly as 'spiral circle, 6 incs' except on a set of 5 needles, so holding the sts on 4 needles, increasing at beg and middle of each needle, and knitting with the 5th.
With these extra increases, this will lie flat in stocking st.

'SHORT ROW' CIRCLES.

Instead of starting in the centre, these circles are knitted sideways, in segments.

Instructions for fine (antique) cotton mat illustrated:

SEGMENT 1

Cast on sts for the radius of the circle, and working in garter st, knit 2 rows.
* Row 3) right-side facing, knit to last st, turn, knit back
Row 5) knit to last 2 sts, turn, knit back.
Cont in this way, leaving 1 more st behind every right-side row, until you have 1 st left, and all the rest held on the needle.

SEGMENT 2

Knit all the sts again, knit 1 row back and begin again from *.

This mat has 6 segments, and a strong spiral design. If it had been knitted in stocking st, the segments would have been longer, and maybe fewer segments would have made a circle. The advantage of this method is that you don't need to plan: the circle is finished when it lies flat.

The heavy striped mat illustrated, knitted in linen 'string', has narrower segments, as 3 sts were left every right-side row rather than 1.

The small woollen sample is knitted similarly, working a straight (striped) section for 12 rows, and then short rows leaving 2 sts behind each time. This creates an 'edge' at the top of the curved section, and can be used to shape garments.

TUBULAR OR DOUBLE-CLOTH KNITTING [ ] –.

Cast on an even no of sts, in 'invisible' cast on, with stitches in alternate colours. Use circular or double-ended needles, as sts have to be slid back and knitted in the same direction on alternate rows.
Slip all sts purlwise.
Row 1) col A * K1, yf, S1, yb, rep from * to end
Row 2) don't turn the knitting: knit again in the same direction: col B, * yb, S1, yf, P1: rep from * to end
Turn work, crossing or linking yarns round each other (otherwise you will have 2 separate pieces).
Row 3) col B, as row 1, don't turn
Row 4) col A, as row 2.
Rep these 4 rows to produce a 'double' fabric, a different colour each side.

It is slow to knit, as only half the stitches are knitted in each row.

This is a good stitch for any item that needs to lie flat, for instance scarves or ties, where the reversible colouring could also be used.

It could be used to create a pocket or similar effect within a piece of knitting, dividing the sts onto different needles for casting off the top of the pocket.

INTERLINKED DIAMONDS /.

This is a way of building a fabric by knitting units that link together as they are knitted. They are shaped by decreasing in the centre of every right-side row, which bends the rows into a right angle: lots of potential here for designs using stripes.

DIAMOND UNIT:
Cast on sts for base (= 2 sides) of diamond: 31 sts.
Row 1) knit
Row 2) knit
Row 3) and all right-side rows, decrease at centre: K14, S2 tog knitwise, K1, p2sso, K14
Row 4) knit, purling the centre st
Row 5) K13, S2, K1, p2sso, K13
Row 6) knit, purling the centre st.
Cont in this way, until there are 3 sts left, S2, K1, p2sso, and fasten off st. Work enough individual diamond shapes for the base of your design, then make the next row by picking up sts from 2 previous diamonds: pick up 15 sts along edge of diamond, pick up 1 st from tip of diamond, pick up 15 sts along edge of next diamond, and make as before.

Decide which decrease to use for the effect you want. If you have a centre st and decrease on either side, the decrease will be less sharp and pointed than the decrease described above.

Introducing stripes to emphasize the structure gives scope for lots of design ideas.

Each diamond could be a different colour or design, or all could be the same.

Shapes can be built from a zig-zag base, or diagonally from one corner (*see* p.75, top).

The fabric produced has a diagonal structure, like a 'bias' fabric, and so will hang well and feel good to wear.

As in previous examples, different stitches make differently shaped diamonds; stocking st will make longer, thinner diamonds.

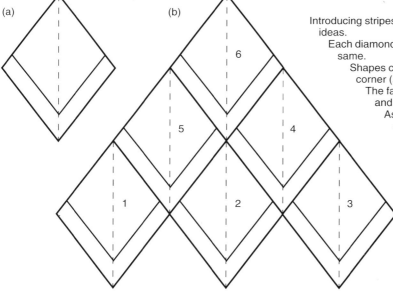

(a)   (b)

Steps for making interlinked diamonds.

INTERLINKED DIAMONDS GROUPED TO MAKE A SQUARE.

In this case, nos 2, 4, 3 and 6 (that is, the outside edges) have half the stitches picked up from neighbouring blocks, and half cast on. Nos 5, 7, 8 and 9 have all stitches picked up.

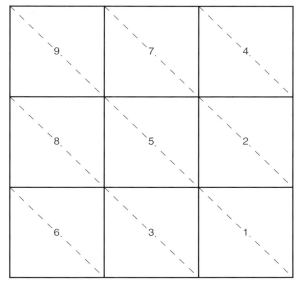

Steps for making interlinked diamonds.

LEFT: INTERLINKED 'SCALLOPS' /.

This works in the same way as the interlinked diamonds, but forming a scale-like pattern with a wavy edge. The decreases are spread across the shape, making the rows curve instead of bending sharply.

1ST SCALLOP
Cast on 29 sts, knit 4 rows.
1st decreasing row: K2 tog, * K4, S2 (slip these sts tog, knitwise), K1, p2sso*, rep to last 6 sts, ending K4, S1, K1, psso.
Working in stocking stitch, decrease every 4th row: next time there will be just 2 K sts between the decs.
3rd dec row will have no sts bet the decs, ending with 5 sts.
Work 3 more rows as before.
Next right-side row: K1, S2, K1, p2sso, K1. Purl back, then K3 tog and fasten off.
As with the diamonds, make several scallops for your base then pick up sts and fill in between.

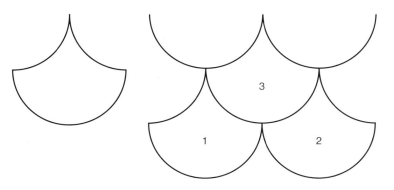

Steps for making interlinked 'scallops'.

4 KNITTING WITH COLOUR

Coloured patterns can be made by knitting with one colour at a time, or two or more in each row for different groups of stitches. Colours can make their own patterns on a plain (for instance, stocking stitch) ground, or they can work with the movement of the stitches in textured, lace or bias stitches, emphasizing the movement or pattern that is already in the structure.

Because using one colour at a time is simpler and easier to manage than carrying several colours in a row, we are looking first at the range of possibilities for making a pattern in coloured stripes, that can then be manipulated by using different stitches to disguise or alter the effect of the stripes and make coloured patterns.

STRIPES

Following the structure of knitting, it is straightforward to knit horizontal stripes, changing colour every one, two or more rows. If you are working back and forth in rows, changing colour at the beginning of right-side rows (for instance in stripes of even numbers of rows), yarns can be left hanging at the end of the row and picked up again when needed. However, if you are working in odd numbers of rows, or changing colour every row, the yarn may be the

wrong end of the row to pick up. In this case, if you use a double-ended or circular needle, the stitches can be slid back to where the yarn is, and the row knitted in the same direction again (*see* p.13, top).

If you are knitting in the round on several needles or a circular needle in stripes, the yarn will always be available at the

OPPOSITE PAGE:
Colour studies.

STRIPES.
To work 1 row of each colour, carrying the colours up the side of the knitting, use double-ended (or circular) needles, so instead of turning the work, if the desired yarn is at the 'wrong' end of the row, slide the stitches back and knit or purl accordingly.

To work 2 rows of each colour, the yarns will always be the same end of the row, and can be carried up the side.

Stepped stripes in circular knitting.

beginning of a round, as there is no end to the row. However, as the construction in this case is spiral, there will always be a step up at the colour change. This is more noticeable in thick yarn, as the step is the depth of one row, so the size of the step depends on the thickness of the yarn. It will also show more in narrow than in wide stripes (so more rows show the step less). So, for example, if you were knitting a striped jumper in the round, there would be a slight mark or step on one side at the colour change, and you might decide it would look better to knit the back and front separately and join at the sides so that the stripes can be matched exactly in the sewing of the seam.

As stripes show up and emphasize the direction of the rows, they can be used to great effect if you are knitting flat pieces from the centre outwards (or the outside edge inwards) in a square or circular shape. Although this may seem an obvious form of pattern making, it need not look simplistic: where the knitting construction is already interesting, stripes make a strong impact and the simplicity can become sophisticated (*see* pp.22, 69 and 70).

If you want your design to have vertical or diagonal stripes, it is worth considering knitting in a different direction: for example for vertical stripes, if these were knitted in several colours, several balls of yarn would be needed for each row. If the piece is knitted sideways so the stripes can still follow the rows, you save having to use several colours in a row, and work each stripe in its own colour one at a time. Similarly for diagonal stripes, if you knit from the bottom edge with lots of colours, again you have the problem of several balls of yarn travelling in each row, but you could build the shape by starting in the corner so that the rows travel diagonally, increasing at either end of the row until you have enough stitches, then decreasing at one or both edges to make the shape you want, with the stripes following the rows.

These suggestions are all searching for the easiest way of achieving a visual effect: however, the feel and texture will also be affected by the different constructions: one colour at a time results in a finer and smoother fabric than using two or more colours in a row, and the tension can also alter with more than one colour per row, so this has to be anticipated, and the number of stitches altered if necessary.

DIAGONAL STRIPES.

Using 2 rows of each colour, knit as 'diagonal square', increasing 1 st at beg of every row until there are enough sts.

To knit a straight-sided piece, continue increasing at one edge, and decrease correspondingly at the other edge on alternate rows.

When it is long enough, decrease at both ends of the row, either by decreasing 1 st at beg of every row, or at either end of alternate rows.

This is a way of making diagonal stripes while working simply, with 1 colour at a time.

DIAGONAL STRIPES USING 'FAIR ISLE' TECHNIQUE.

Here, 2 colours are used in every row, although the colours both change periodically. With 2 stitches in each colour, they are stepped sideways 1 st every row, making diagonal stripes.

This makes a thicker, firmer fabric than the previous sample, and the structure is vertical, not on the bias.

MOSS ST STRIPES ^ < > –.

With 2 rows knitted in each colour, moss st (K1, P1) disguises and blurs the colours.

DIFFERENT STITCHES, STRIPES.

ABOVE: 2-row stripes are worked in vertical panels of stocking st, reverse stocking st, and moss st, to compare the blending of the colours.

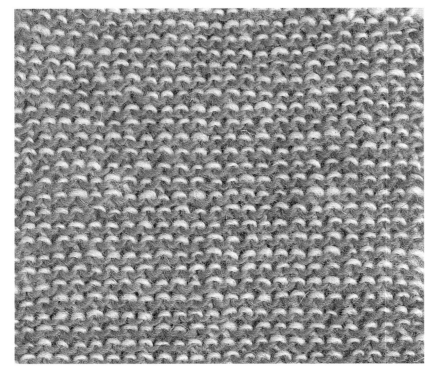

GARTER ST STRIPES ^ [ ] –.
1 row of each colour worked in garter st makes an even, all-over fleck rather than a stripe, with the flecks having a different direction on each side.

Knitting in stocking st, this is worked similarly to the textured short rows (*see* p.64 and also p.83).

After knitting 6 rows of stocking stitch, change colour. The example illustrated uses a random-dyed yarn for the short rows, as the colour changes in the yarn show the direction of the rows more clearly.

K11, turn, S1 P6, turn, S1 K4, turn, S1 P2, turn, S1 K3, turn, S1 P5, turn, S1 K along the row to start making the next short row section.

When there are short row 'bulges' all the way along the row, change colour and knit another band of stocking st.

On this sample, the next row of 'bulges' fits in between the first row, balancing the design.

These short-row sections are made in the same way as turning a sock heel, and do in fact create a bulge, rather than lying flat. This can be as pronounced as you like, depending on the number of sts left behind each time you turn; that is, if only 1 st is left at each turn, the shape will be more pronounced and three-dimensional. With this in mind, it is possible to make distorted, undulating fabric even in plain stocking st, and more texture can be added using other stitches.

BELOW: A practical use of short rows for shaping a heel.

DIFFERENT STITCHES

Working stripes in stocking stitch gives a clean colour change on the knit side of the fabric, and a mixed or blurred colour change on the purl side. We are used to calling these differences 'right' and 'wrong' sides, but of course the different characteristics can be used as part of a design.

Because the purl stitch makes the loops of the upper and lower stitch cross each other when they link, the colours are visually mixed; so if you want a soft, mixed effect from your stripes, the purl side of stocking stitch could be used, or a moss stitch, where stitches are alternately knitted and purled in each row. Moss stitch worked in one-row stripes blends the colours very subtly, and it also softens the edges of two-row stripes.

Blocks of knit and purl-side stocking stitch or moss stitch can provide alternating clear and mixed stripes.

Garter stitch also makes an unexpected pattern worked in stripes of one colour to each row, and if worked in two-row stripes, again has a hard-edge and a blurred side.

ZIG-ZAG STRIPES /.

Cast on a multiple of 8 sts, + 2 edge sts.
K 2 rows.
Row 1) K1, M1 * K2, S2, K1, p2sso, K2, M1, K1, M1 *, rep to end
Row 2) purl.
Rep these 2 rows, with 4 rows in darker colour, and 2 row stripes of lighter colour.

Because the sts are pushed into a slanting direction, this fabric behaves like a bias fabric.

LACY STRIPES, TRAVELLING VINE O /.

Cast on a multiple of 8 sts + 4 edge sts.
Row 1) K2, * O, K1B, O, K2 tog B, K5, rep from *, K2
Row 2) P2, * P4, P2 tog B, P3, rep from *, P2
Row 3) K2, * O, K1B, O, K2, K2 tog B, K3, rep from *, K2
Row 4) P2, * P2, P2 tog B, P5, rep from *, P2
Row 5) K2, * K1B, O, K4, K2 tog B, K1, O, rep from *, K2
Row 6) P2, * P1, P2 tog B, P6, rep from *, P2
Row 7) K2, * K5, K2 tog, O, K1B, O, rep from *, K2
Row 8) P2, * P3, P2 tog, P4, rep from *, P2
Row 9) K2, * K3, K2 tog, K2, O, K1B, O, rep from *, K2
Row 10) P2 * P5, P2 tog, P2, rep from *, P2
Row 11) K2, * O, K1, K2 tog, K4, O, K1B, rep from *, K2
Row 12) P2, *P6, P2 tog, P1, rep from *, P2.

If coloured stripes are used in this pattern, they differ according to where they cross the pattern.

There are two distinct movements, to the right and to the left: the direction changes on rows 1 and 7.

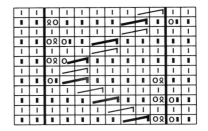

WAVY STRIPES, 'OLD SHALE' O /.
Cast on stitches divisible by 11.
Row 1) col A * K2 tog, K2 tog, O, K1, O, K1, O, K1,
O, K2 tog, K2 tog * rep
Row 2) col A, purl
Row 3) col B, knit
Row 4) col B, knit.
In this traditional lace pattern, 4 incs balance 4 decs
within Row 1. Larger groups of incs and decs would
make larger waves, incs and decs every 2 rows
would make steeper waves, or used less frequently
would make more gradual waves.

SHORT ROWS

Changing colour when knitting in short rows (*see* Chapter 3) would make distorted stripes, showing up the structure of the knitting. If the placing of the short row areas is random, colours could emphasize the meandering character of the rows. Alternatively the short-row areas could be worked in a contrasting colour to the plain areas in an organized way to make repeating patterns. In whatever way the short rows are used, colours could be added in stripes to accentuate the movement of the rows, and to enhance the design.

LACY STITCHES, BIAS KNITTING

When increases and decreases are used within rows, stitches begin to move up and down, in waves and zig-zags, as we saw in Chapter 3. Here is a great opportunity for working in coloured stripes to highlight these movements. Some traditional lace stitches have a strong shaping and emphasis when worked in a single colour that can be completely changed and even contradicted by working in bands of different colours: stitches like 'travelling vine', 'falling leaf', and other busy lacy patterns can produce unexpected wavy stripes. More obvious patterns that work successfully in stripes are 'old shale' or 'feather and fan', and all zig-zag patterns. These can be worked on large or small scales (with few or many stitches between the shapings), and in soft, muted colours, or strong contrasts. There are endless possibilities here, and it is fascinating (and possibly addictive) to spend time experimenting with these stitches.

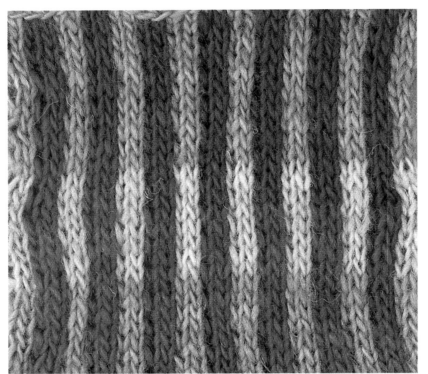

SLIP ST STRIPES > < ^.
Vertical stripes made by knitting 1 colour per row.
Multiple of 4 sts.
Using col A, knit 1 row, purl 1 row.
Row 1) col B, K3, S2 * K2, S2, rep from * to last 3 sts, K3
Row 2) col B, P3, S2 * P2, S2, rep from * to last 3 sts, P3
Row 3) col A, K1, S2 * K2, S2, rep from * to last st, K1
Row 4) col A, P1, S2, * P2, S2, rep from * to last st, P1.
Rep these 4 rows.

I	S	S	I	I	S	S	I
I	**S**	**S**	**I**	**I**	**S**	**S**	**I**
I	I	I	S	S	I	I	I
I	**I**	**I**	**S**	**S**	**I**	**I**	**I**

SLIP STITCHES

With slip stitches, the striped effect of working in rows of different colours can be lost or disguised, and so there is great scope for making colour patterns while still working in this simple way with one colour at a time. Again the structure was described in Chapter 3, but by changing colours, the action of slipping stitches of one colour across a row of a different colour makes it possible to create small repeating geometric patterns and textures.

TEA COSY IN DYED AND SPACE-DYED WOOL, USING TRADITIONAL STITCH, K6, S6. > < ^ [ ] |.

—	S	S	S	S	S	—	—	—	—	—	—
I	**S**	**S**	**S**	**S**	**S**	**I**	**I**	**I**	**I**	**I**	**I**
—	—	—	—	—	—	S	S	S	S	S	S
I	**I**	**I**	**I**	**I**	**I**	**S**	**S**	**S**	**S**	**S**	**I**
—	S	S	S	S	S	—	—	—	—	—	—
I	**S**	**S**	**S**	**S**	**S**	**I**	**I**	**I**	**I**	**I**	**I**
—	—	—	—	—	—	S	S	S	S	S	S
I	**I**	**I**	**I**	**I**	**I**	**S**	**S**	**S**	**S**	**S**	**I**

The patterns are usually more success-ful if they are regular and repetitive, firstly because it is easy to lose the plot with slip stitches and forget which stage of the pat-tern you are at, so a regular pattern enables you to count and repeat more eas-ily. Secondly, slipping the stitches does distort the fabric, pulling the slipped stitches up across the rows, and also pulling in slightly where the yarn is carried across the slipped stitches, so a regular pattern makes for an even texture. A 'ran-dom' pattern would in fact have to be carefully considered and planned to make sure that the result looked intentional, and not a random accident.

Slip stitch is also a simple way of knit-ting vertical stripes while only using one colour at a time. For example, the sample shown at the top of p.84 could have been knitted with two stitches to each colour in a 'Fair Isle' technique, both colours used through each row. In fact this piece has been worked in one colour at a time, slip-ping the stitches, which is slower than Fair Isle to knit, as only half the stitches are knitted each row, but saves having to han-dle two colours per row. There is also a

SLIP ST MOSAIC > < ^ – |.
Multiple of 6 sts + 2.
Instructions are given for 2 colours, light (L) and dark (D). In the sample, the lights and darks vary.
Slip stitches purlwise, and always carry yarn on wrong side.
Row 1) col D, knit
Row 2) col D, purl
Row 3) col L, K6, S1 * K5, S1, rep from * to last st, K1
Row 4) col L, P1, * S1, P5 rep from * to last st, P1
Row 5) col D, * K1, S1, K3, S1, rep from * to last 2 sts, K2
Row 6) col D, P2, S1, P3, S1 * P1, S1, P3, S1, rep from * to last st, P1
Row 7) col L, K4, S1, K1, S1, * K3, S1, K1, S1, rep from * to last st, K1
Row 8) col L, P1 * S1, P1, S1, P3, rep from * to last st, P1
Row 9) col D, * K3, S1, K1, S1, rep from * to last 2 sts, K2
Row 10) col D, P2 * S1, P1, S1, P3, rep from * to end
Row 11) col L, K4, S1 * K5, S1, rep from * to last 3 sts, K3
Row 12) col L, P3, S1 * P5, S1, rep from * to last 4 sts, P4.

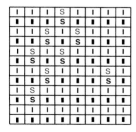

'BASKET WEAVE' SLIP ST SQUARES

\> < ^ – |.

Multiple of 12 sts , +7.
D=dark
L=light
Row 1) col D (right side) knit
Row 2) col D, P1 * K5, P1, rep from * to end
Row 3) col L, K2, S1, (K1, S1) × 2, K5 * S1, (K1, S1) × 3, K5, rep from * to last 7 sts, S1, (K1, S1) × 2, K2
Row 4) col L, P2, S1 (P1, S1) × 2, K5 * S1, (P1, S1) × 3, K5, rep from * to last 7 sts, S1 (P1, S1) × 2, P2
Row 5) col D (K1, S1) × 3, * K7, S1 (K1, S1) × 2, rep from * to last st, K1
Row 6) col D (P1, S1) × 3, P1, * K5, P1 (S1 P1) × 3, rep from * to end.
Rep last 4 rows once more.
Row 11) as row 3
Row 12) as row 4
Row 13) as row 1
Row 14) as row 2
Row 15) col L, K6, S1 (K1, S1) × 3, * K5, S1, (K1, S1) × 3, rep from * to last 6 sts, K6
Row 16) col L, P1 K5 * S1 (P1, S1) × 3, K5, rep from * to last st, P1
Row 17) col D, K7 * S1, (K1, S1) × 2, K7, rep from * to end
Row 18) col D, P1, K5, P1 *(S1, P1) × 3, K5, P1, rep from * to end.
Rep the last 4 rows once more.
Row 23) as row 15
Row 24) as row 16.
These 24 rows form the pattern.

difference in texture, more evident if wider stripes are worked in this way. The traditional tea-cosy stitch illustrated on p.84 has 6 stitches per stripe, so is 'knit 6, slip 6': if this had been worked with the two colours along the same row, that is, 'knit 6 col A, knit 6 col B', it would have made a flatter fabric, as it is the slipping of the 6 stitches that pulls it in widthways, creating the ridges, and therefore providing the thick, heat-trapping character of this stitch.

SLIP ST DIAMOND TRELLIS > < ^ [ ].
Slip stitches purlwise, and always carry yarn on
wrong side.
Rep of 14 sts: for this sample, add 2 edge sts and
cast on 16.
Use 2 colours. In the sample col A is plain, and col B
is variegated.
Row 1) col B, knit
Row 2) col B, purl
Row 3) col A, K1 * S2, K10, S2 * rep to end, K1
Row 4) col A, K1 * S2, K10, S2 * rep to end, K1
Rows 5 and 6) as 1 and 2
Row 7) col A, K1 * K1, S2, K8, S2, K1 * rep to end, K1
Row 8) col A, K1 * K1, S2, K8, S2, K1 * rep to end, K1
Rows 9 and 10) as 1 and 2
Row 11) col A, K1 * K2, S2, K6, S2, K2 * rep to end, K1
Row 12) col A, K1 * K2, S2, K6, S2, K2 * rep to end, K1
Row 13 and 14) as 1 and 2
Row 15) col A, K1 * K3, S2, K4, S2, K3 * rep to end, K1

Row 16) col A, K1 * K3, S2, K4, S2, K3 * rep to end, K1
Rows 17 and 18) as 1 and 2
Row 19) col A, K1 * K4, S2, K2, S2, K4 * rep to end, K1
Row 20) col A, K1 * K4, S2, K2, S2, K4 * rep to end, K1
Rows 21 and 22) as 1 and 2
Row 23) col A, K1 * K5, S4, K5 * rep to end, K1
Row 24) col A, K1 * K5, S4, K5 * rep to end, K1
Rows 25 and 26) as 1 and 2
Rows 27 and 28) as 19 and 20
Rows 29 and 30) as 1 and 2
Rows 31 and 32) as 15 and 16
Rows 33 and 34) as 1 and 2
Rows 35 and 36) as 11 and 12
Rows 37 and 38) as 1 and 2
Rows 39 and 40) as 7 and 8
Rows 41 and 42) as 1 and 2
Rows 43 and 44) as 3 and 4.
These 44 rows form the pattern.

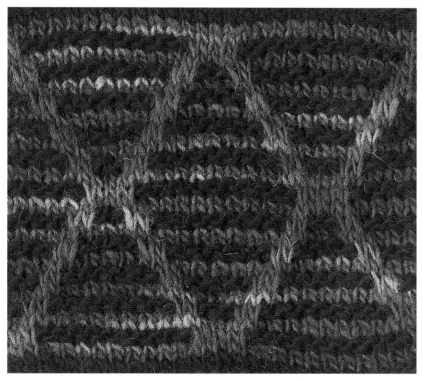

Sometimes slip-stitch patterns are described as 'mosaics', as small interlocking geometric and tessellating patterns can be knitted in this method very effectively. However, it is also possible to make large-scale patterns by using the slipped unit at regular intervals, and moving it gradually across to build squares, diagonals or diamond shapes that could be almost any size. So if small textural patterns do not appeal, look at the possibilities for building larger patterns, combining texture, colour, and ease of knitting.

MIXING COLOUR

Another use of slip-stitch patterns is to mix colour within the knitting. We have the opportunity in constructive textile techniques such as weaving, crochet and knitting, to build colour into the fabric as it is made, using the stitch as a small dot of colour. This means that if we want to make a coloured area, for example red, we are not bound to use one shade of red only, but can combine lots of different shades to make a richer, more interesting colour. If you look at the colour of brick, or of roof tiles, the general effect might be a strong terracotta colour. If you look more closely, there will be a lot of variation brought about by perhaps uneven qualities in the clay or the firing process: perhaps by staining and weathering or the growth of lichens on the surface. All these make for a richer or perhaps gentler overall colour that remains interesting the closer you look. This is also possible with creating textiles and with knitting: if you are going to the trouble of making something by hand, it is more rewarding if it is not only interesting or striking from a distance, but more detail is revealed and the interest grows as you look more closely.

Slip stitches have the ability to mix up colours that have been knitted separately in rows, crossing them over each other so that from a distance the colours blur, rather like small dots of colour in an Impressionist painting. So for example, shades of green, or the illusion of green could be built out of rows of blues and yellows, or greeny-blues and greeny-yellows, where the colours have been 'mixed' by the use of stitches.

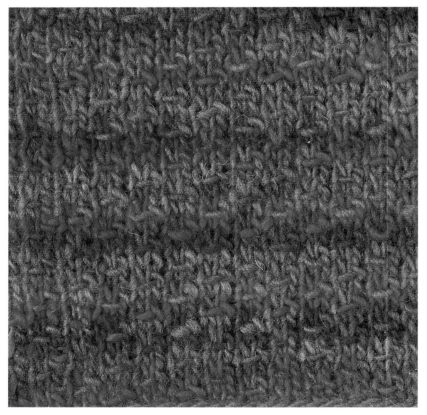

FLECKED TWEED > < ^ [] – |.
Multiple of 4 sts, +3 sts.
A variety of colours are used in this sample, changing colour every 2 rows.
    Instructions are given for 2 colours over 4 rows, but they could be a different 2 each time.
Row 1) (wrong side) col A, P1, yb, S1, yf * P3, yb, S1, yf; rep from * to last st, P1
Row 2) col A, K1, S1,* K3, S1; rep from * to last st, K1
Row 3) col B, P3 * yb, S1, yf, P3; rep from * to end
Row 4) col B, K3 * S1, K3; rep from * to end.

GARTER SLIP ST > < ^ [] – |.

Multiple of 2 sts + 1.
Slip stitches purlwise, and always carry yarn on wrong side.
R = rust, Y = yellow
Row 1) col R, knit (right side)
Row 2) col R, knit
Row 3) col Y, K1 * S1, K1, rep to end
Row 4) col Y, K1 * S1, K1, rep to end.
Rep these 4 rows.

SPECKLE RIB > < ^ [] – |.

Multiple of 2 sts, +1.
Slip stitches purlwise, and always carry yarn on wrong side.
R = rusts, Y = yellows: 3 different shades of rust and 3 different shades of yellow are used in the sample.
Row 1) col R, knit
Row 2) col R, purl
Row 3) col Y, K1 * S1, K1, rep from * to end
Row 4) col Y, K1 * S1, K1, rep from * to end
Row 5) col R, knit
Row 6) col R, purl
Row 7) col Y, K2 * S1, K1, rep to last 2 sts, K2
Row 8) col Y, K2 * S1, K1, rep to last 2 sts, K2.
Rep these 8 rows.

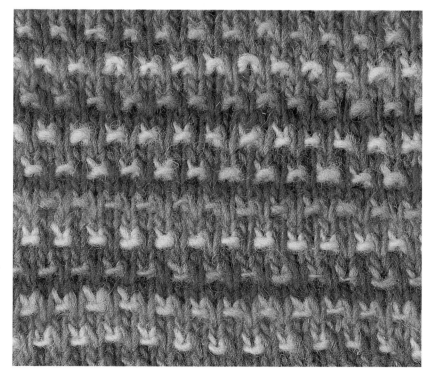

'FAIR ISLE' OR 'JACQUARD'

This is a way of knitting with colours, which made the Scottish islands famous, but as the usually small geometric patterns

Knitting Fair Isle with yarn in each hand.

BELOW: Yarns woven in on reverse of Fair Isle knitting.

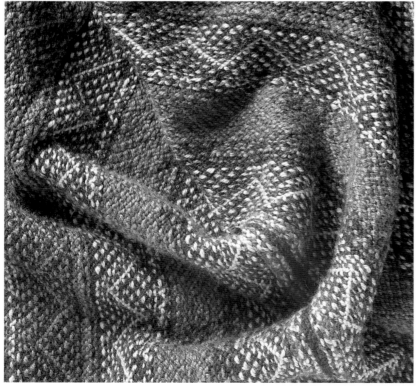

produced look similar to those produced by weaving on a Jacquard loom, both names are used for geometric coloured patterns. To keep things simple, in this book it will be called Fair Isle knitting.

Traditionally only two colours are used in each row, although these colours could be changed any amount of times during the knitting, sometimes keeping the background plain throughout, and sometimes with all colours varying. The patterns are easily charted on graph paper, with each square representing 1 stitch, and worked in stocking stitch, with a few stitches worked alternately in each colour. The yarn not being knitted is carried on the back of the work, either stranded across, or woven into the second yarn as it goes. Limiting the number of colours to two makes it much easier to knit. The weight of the fabric is also affected: two colours obviously make a thicker fabric than one, but any more than two can become very bulky.

The separate yarns are often carried on different fingers of the right hand. It can be almost as quick to knit with two colours as with one if the yarns are arranged on different fingers and don't need to be dropped and picked up each time they are needed. Another very efficient way of knitting two colours is to carry one in each hand, knitting right- and left-handed. With an extra twiddle between stitches, the second yarn is woven over the first between stitches, and a beautiful evenly tensioned fabric is knitted. If you intend to do much Fair Isle knitting and are prepared to learn a new technique, even if it takes a week of regular practice, the resulting speed and evenness makes it worth while.

Leaving the yarn stranded across the back of the knitting can affect the tension of the fabric: the horizontal stretch is limited by these straight strands. If the yarn is woven up and down at the back, and is not pulled tight but allowed to travel at its own tension, this 'up and down' movement allows a little more give or stretch than stranding. It also means that it is more like a woven fabric, more substantial and firm, and there are no long loops or strands that can catch and pull.

This kind of colour knitting lends itself to small repeating patterns or small regular motifs simply because if two colours are travelling across the row, it seems logical to use them both at regular intervals: but the gaps between colours can be as long as you are prepared to 'weave' the yarn. The only reason for the regularity is again ease of knitting: the knitter can easily cope with a regular rhythm of, for example, 'four, six,

INSTRUCTIONS FOR KNITTING FAIR ISLE WITH TWO HANDS

Use two colours, holding one in each hand, with yarn over the forefingers, and once round little fingers to give it tension and keep it in place.

There are four movements, two for the knit row and two for the purl. The instructions are given for weaving in on alternate sts, but the spare yarn could be woven in every second or third st.

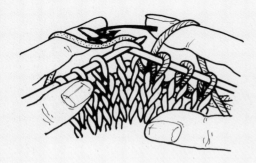

(1) *Knit row, RH knitting, LH weaving:*
a) K st with RH, holding LH yarn below
b) K next st with RH, holding LH yarn above.
Rep a) and b).

(3) *Purl row, RH purling, LH weaving:*
a) purl st with RH, holding LH yarn below
b) purl next st with RH, holding LH yarn above.
Rep a) and b).

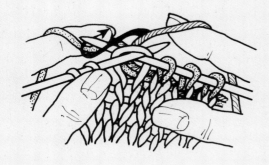

(2) *Knit row, LH knitting, RH weaving:*
a) K st with LH
b) needle in next st: RH yarn over as if to knit, LH yarn over
   RH yarn off, and make stitch (say 'over, over, off, through'). Rep a) and b).

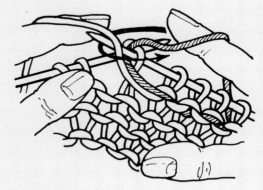

(4) *Purl row, LH purling, RH weaving:*
a) Purl st with LH (note: yarn must go in same direction over needle as it does in RH purling)
b) needle in next st, RH yarn under needle, LH yarn over needle, RH yarn off, and make st (say 'under, over, off, through'). Rep a) and b).

Intarsia.

Back of intarsia.

two, six' or whatever, without having to concentrate too hard. It is equally successful to work something irregular such as lettering or script, or pictorial patterning, it just needs more attention.

The potential problems to look out for in Fair Isle knitting are:

◆ the tension must be even and not too tight, or the fabric can feel buckled and unpleasant

◆ the 'woven' yarn may show through to the front of the knitting, especially in a smooth yarn such as a mercerized cotton; this can influence the colour of the pattern: it can be attractive, but needs to be considered.

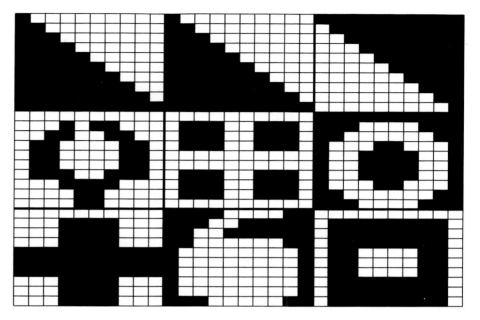

Chart for intarsia.

INTARSIA

Intarsia knitting is different from Fair Isle in that the colours do not travel all the way along the row, but each colour keeps to its own area, linking with the neighbouring colour to prevent holes or gaps.

This opens up the possibility of working in larger areas of each colour, in a much freer way; and of using as many colours as you like in a row.

The resulting fabric is less heavy than Fair Isle, as it is only the weight of single-colour knitting. The colours may also be clearer and brighter, as there is no different coloured yarn being carried or woven across.

The difficulties to look out for in intarsia knitting are as follows.

◆ Because of the freedom of the technique, there is much more skill involved in making the design successful artistically: any design, landscape, picture, or abstract can be knitted, and if it is not well-drawn, balanced and considered, that is how it will look.

◆ The joining between colours needs to be very carefully done or can spoil the whole design. To link colours together, twist neighbouring yarns once round each other at every join. This is most noticeable if there is a vertical join, as it would result in a vertical slit or opening if not linked.

◆ If different types of yarns are used, there is a danger that the fabric may become lumpy and uneven: the weight of the different yarns needs to be balanced, or alternatively, the lumpiness has to look as if it is intentional.

◆ It is not possible to work intarsia knitting in the round, as the yarns will be left at the wrong end of each area of colour, and need to be worked back from the other end, so it has to be knitted back and forth.

5 DESIGNING AND CALCULATING

WORKING OUT A DESIGN

Designing does not have to be complicated. There are several elements to a finished garment or item that give it character and individuality: the shape, the materials, and the quality of the fabric all contribute to the whole. If the shape is kept simple, there can be emphasis on pattern or colour to make it individual, or on the other hand the colour and stitch could be plain and all the interest could be in shaping and construction. Often the most successful designs are very simple, with the success lying in the quality of materials. Some couture designers have succeeded in creating clothes that are classics and can look good through several generations of fashion changes, and others may achieve exciting looks that are stunning but short-lived. The aim is up to the designer.

Anyone can make their own design, whether it is a plain-shaped jumper in a plain stitch, or a complicated intricate shape in multi-coloured and textured patterns: the satisfaction is in knowing that it is yours. Adapting and imitating are ways of beginning to make your own variations, and there is nothing wrong with being influenced by either contemporary or past designs.

If you are prepared to have a go, there are several ways of arriving at a design, whether it is for something to wear, a furnishing fabric or cushion, or a knitted object. There are no rules, only guidelines, and different methods suit different people. Some people are inspired by colours, textures or patterns that they have seen, and others are excited by particular yarns, constructions and shapes. Sometimes an idea can leap out and grab you, and at other times it may be a hard, long-drawn-out process, developing and selecting ideas. Some people are comfortable working on paper, sketching, using coloured crayons or paints, exploring visual effects, while others may prefer to explore through the material and the technique by playing with yarn, and knitting samples. Often both approaches will take a part in the process.

Adapting an existing design is a simple way to start, but if you are designing from scratch it takes time that is often in short supply, and there are a few short cuts to help you make necessary decisions that are part of the process of designing.

Looking, Seeing and Analysing

You may find that you often see colour combinations that strike you as attractive, beautiful, or inspiring; but later find it difficult to remember the exact grouping, or why it was so appealing. The first step is to look again, and try to analyse what you see. It may at first be a particular shade of a colour that has caught your attention, so the next stage is to look at what this colour is next to: is there a large or small area of it, and what are you seeing it against? It may be only a small amount of a particularly vivid colour. Is it looking so vivid because it is next to a large, quiet colour, perhaps complementary to it? For example, the sky at sunset may be quite a small area of rich reds, oranges and pinks, seen against an expanse of clear turquoise-blue or deep indigo. As blue and orange are complementary in the colour spectrum, they 'set each other off'. Red poppies look more vivid against a field of green than do white or blue flowers, for the same reason.

OPPOSITE PAGE:
Colour studies.

Another example might be a kilim rug with rich blue and terracotta colours, heightened by small amounts of black or white. It is often the proportions of the colours that are significant in producing the effect.

There are various ways of noting down colour combinations, and if it is something you have not done before, you may not think it necessary, but in fact making notes also helps you to look more closely, to see and notice more, and to remember better, and eventually to understand what is attracting you, and why. One way is to note your observations down in a sketchbook. If you are used to this method it is easy and obvious, and can be extremely helpful. Paints or crayons, pastels, oil pastels, or water-based crayons can all be good; or perhaps torn paper used in collage is more accessible than drawing or painting materials, and will also give a density of colour that might be more comparable to the

Yarn windings to study proportions of colours, and knitted samples.

intensity and depth of coloured yarn than working by colouring onto white paper.

Another way of working is to move straight into yarns, and make a 'yarn wrapping'. For this you will need a piece of card, double-sided sticky tape, and as much choice of coloured yarns as possible. If the tape is laid in a strip along one side of the card, it will provide an adhesive area that will hold the ends of the yarn firmly in place.

Look at your chosen colours, and find yarns that represent them as closely as possible. Now simplify what you see into bands or stripes of the different colours, following the proportions as accurately as possible, and noticing what is next to what, including the tones: light and dark can be significant in setting colours off, or heightening the effect. If there is a spotty or textured area, simplify it at this stage into fine stripes or lines, maybe only one thread wide, to try to achieve the mixture and proportions that you have seen. If the colours are difficult to match, or richer and more varied than the yarns you have, mix the yarns to approximate and build the colour: for instance, an orange could be mixed from strands of reds and yellows. Wind the yarns carefully, covering the card completely so that the density of the coloured yarn is not diluted by card showing through. Then pin it up and look from a distance. If your original inspiration was in a photo or picture, or you are working from your sketchbook, put this up next to it, and assess what you have seen, and how you have translated it.

Now start knitting, again following the sequence of colours in the yarn winding, but also looking at the areas of mixed colour, and finding stitches to mix colours in the knitting, as suggested in Chapter 4. Mixed colours used next to plain colours can accentuate the brightness of the plain areas.

When you have knitted for a while, have a break: pin up your knitting so that when you come back to it again you see it from a distance first. It is important to look at designs from a distance after working so

Colour studies from guinea fowl feathers: yarn windings, knitted samples and finished jacket.

closely: sometimes the proportions change, and unexpected parts jump out more than you anticipated. You also need to think about scale at this stage. If you are working towards a garment design, think how the scale will work on a person. If it is for an interior, again, imagine the scale *in situ*, and think how designs that are large can dominate and take over from shape and construction. Photocopying is also a way of reproducing the design, and the scale can easily be changed.

A useful time-saving and revealing trick at this stage is to use mirrors: either hold your sample to the edge of a mirror, or put mirrors on either side, and you instantly have a larger area of knitting to assess that will be helpful in trying to visualize your final design. Perhaps the sample of pattern could be scanned into a computer, and proportions, scale or colours changed: use any tools you can think of to help you develop and plan, and to speed up the process of deciding on your design.

The same applies to textured patterns as well as colours. Rather than laboriously trying to draw textured stitches, you could do rubbings on fine paper with wax or oil crayons of any appropriate textures you can find: brick or stone to give fine spots, wood grain, carpet: once you have a selection of stripes and textures that approximate to knitted textures, cut them up and play with them in different arrangements before you start knitting. Textured stitches are usually slower to knit than plain knitting because of the slipping, twisting, crossing over, increasing and decreasing, so once you have knitted a sample, again use mirrors,

A larger impression of a small knitted sample using mirrors.

Rubbings of textured surfaces, and knitted textures.

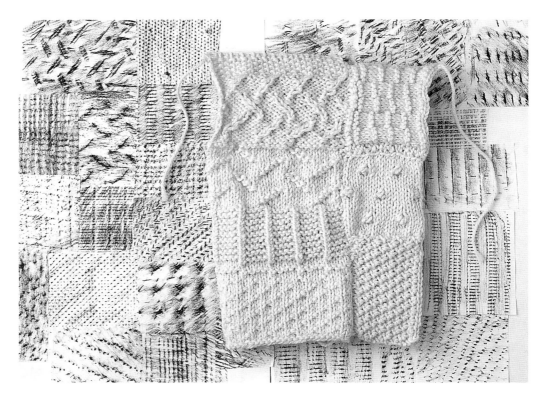

photocopying or computer technology to magnify the area you have knitted.

If you intend to use several different stitches within a design, it will be essential to do a sample of every stitch, to compare the different tensions. It may be possible to use different needle sizes successfully for different stitches in the same yarn, if some pull in more tightly than others. The needle size needs to be explored, seeing how larger needles make looser tension, and how this will affect the look of the knitting, and the way it hangs or drapes. In a plain stocking stitch there is usually an appropriate size of needle to give a happy relationship between yarn and needle, and therefore a fabric that feels neither too tight nor too loopy. Knitting yarns usually indicate the needle size for each yarn on the wrapper, but you need to be aware that this varies according to individual knitters, and be prepared to experiment with other needle sizes. You may not want a 'normal'

fabric or tension, but perhaps something very stiff and tightly knitted, or something slack and transparent: once again, there are no rules, but it must satisfy you as being the right tension for your design.

WORKING IT ALL OUT

Once you have experimented with stitches, explored effects in pattern, colour and texture, knitted endless samples and formed lots of ideas for designs, how do you translate these ideas into a final knitted piece?

There are two major decisions to make, and they both depend on having made a final sample that is knitted in the chosen yarn, stitch and pattern, on the needles that you have decided are right for the job. The design needs to have been sketched or drawn out with all measurements included. The calculations will not be accurate if all decisions have not been finalized.

1) How much yarn will it take?
2) How many stitches are needed to cast on? (and how many rows, increases, decreases, and so on?)

It is tempting to go straight into the final knitting without calculating anything much in advance, because it is seen as wasting time that could be spent getting going on the project. Making it up as you go along and improvising is another approach: the results may be wonderful, or chaotic, or even chaotically wonderful: or it may look like an amateur disaster.

Working it out beforehand eliminates the risk that a) the size will be wrong, or b) the yarn will run out.

If you know beforehand that there is not enough of your (perhaps irreplaceable) yarn, then you can change the design to include other yarns: in effect, you have the freedom to be flexible before you start, rather than being driven into a tight corner and not having the courage to undo all that knitting, and eventually having to make do with something you will never be satisfied with. It may take one hour to knit a sample, but weeks of work to get half-way through a garment heading for disaster.

Calculating the Weight of Yarn

The simple and approximate way to work out the weight of yarn is to weigh a finished garment made in similar yarn. This is a rough guide only, but may be useful.

To work it out more exactly, measure your finished sample, multiply length by width to find out the area of your sample in square centimetres (or inches). Now weigh it as accurately as possible: cookery scales will weigh small amounts.

Next, work out the area of the design you are going to make. On a jumper, the front and back may be quite straightforward rectangular shapes, but the sleeves are usually wider at the top than the cuff.

If you can tackle the mathematics, you can work out the area precisely: otherwise, take an average width measurement about half-way along the length (remembering that the sleeve is folded double), and multiply this by the length for the sleeve area.

Total the areas of front, back, and two sleeves.

The formula for calculating the total weight of yarn is:

area of garment divided by area of sample, multiplied by weight of sample = weight of garment.

This gives you the total yarn for the whole garment: if there are different yarns or colours in the design, you could work out the proportions of different colours by counting the stitches and working out proportions of the weight: alternatively some guessing or estimating may be necessary.

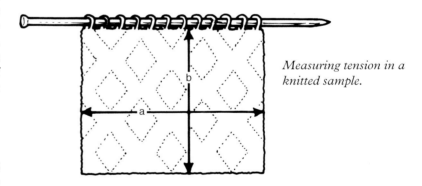

Measuring tension in a knitted sample.

Calculating Stitches

Having knitted a sample of the stitch or stitches to be used:

◆ measure the number of stitches in a width of 10cm (4in);

◆ measure the number of rows in a length of 10cm (4in).

This is really the minimum measurement to be of any use: there is always more room for error in a smaller sample when multiplied into a large piece, so do as large a sample as possible.

To check that your measurement is as accurate as possible, measure each direction in three separate places and take the average. Now look at the measurement of the piece you want to knit. A simple example could be a square cushion to measure 45cm (18in).

This is the formula for working out all measurements into stitches (or rows) (very easy with a calculator):

measurement of item divided by measurement of sample, multiplied by no of sts in sample = no of sts needed.

In our example, if there were 30 sts = 10cm in the knitted sample, and you need to know how many sts for the 45cm cushion, this is the formula:

$$\frac{45}{10} \times 30 = 135 \text{ sts}$$

The next stage is to go back to your sample and see if there is a repeat pattern in the design you have chosen. Supposing your pattern has a 5-st repeat, then 135 sts is fine. However if you have an 8-st repeat, you could adjust it to 136 sts, which is divisible by 8, without changing the size of the cushion too much. If your design is bigger, or will not fit very near to 135 sts, you may need to change or adjust your design, or you could design a border to use up the spare stitches, or work plain knitting round the edge.

To work out how many rows you will need, use the same formula, but notice that the number of rows is different, usually more than the number of stitches, as usually (that is, in stocking stitch) the knitted stitch is wider than it is tall. If our sample has 36 rows = 10cm, then:

$$\frac{45}{10} \times 36 = 162 \text{ rows}$$

This is often not such an urgent calculation as the number of stitches, because you can measure the length as you go: however, if you need to see how your design will fit in lengthways, it may be necessary to know exactly how many rows it will need, and plan accordingly.

CALCULATING STITCHES FOR A JUMPER

This formula for calculating stitches can be applied to any shape, as long as you know the measurements you are aiming for. Here is a way of making a very simply shaped jumper, showing the measurements you will need. It is better to arrive at your measurements by measuring something that is already a good fit, rather than trying to guess from body measurements how much extra to allow for a comfortable fit. On the other hand, for something very close-fitting, use the same plan with actual body measurements, but more measurements will be needed, as the shape will need to increase and decrease for every curve to fit closely, unless a stretchy stitch is used.

A good basic way of knitting a jumper is to make it in one piece. This means there is almost no sewing up, and you have the satisfaction of casting off a finished garment. Traditionally, the Guernsey sweaters were knitted this way in fishing communities around the coasts of Britain. Once the construction is mastered, it can be adapted and adjusted for more complicated shapes.

Take the measurement across the garment, double it, and calculate how many stitches are needed for the whole body.

Example: if your garment is to measure 53cm flat across the body, this would be a total of 106cm all the way round.

If you had knitted a sample with 24 sts = 10cm, this is how you would calculate for the number of stitches required to knit in the round:

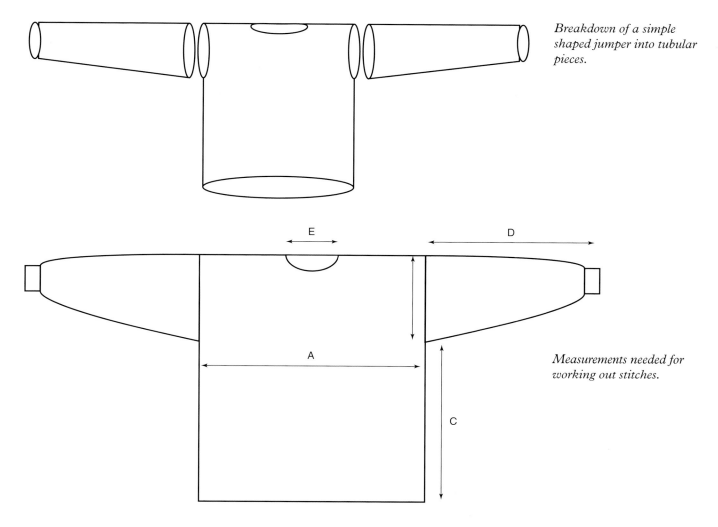

Breakdown of a simple shaped jumper into tubular pieces.

Measurements needed for working out stitches.

$$\frac{106}{10} \times 24 = 254.4$$

If you decided to knit back and front separately, it would be:

$$\frac{53}{10} \times 24 = 127.2$$

Look at your pattern repeat, and decide whether to use 254 sts (or 127 if knitting back and front separately), or whether to have a few more or less to fit the pattern.

Cast On
Cast on stitches for the body onto a circular needle that should be slightly shorter in length than the total measurement. For example, a 100cm length needle will knit a garment bigger than 100cm round.

Welt
Use a stitch appropriate for the welt: if you want it to lie flat, use garter stitch; if you want a curling edge, use stocking stitch, knit or purl side out. If you want the welt to pull in more firmly than the rest of the garment, use a stretchy stitch like ribbing, and possibly smaller sized needles.

Body

Knit the body, round and round, in your chosen pattern, until you reach the armholes.

Back

Put half the sts on a spare circular needle, and continue straight up the back by working back and forth until you reach the shoulders. Leave sts on needle.

Front

Work the front the same, until 10cm shorter than the back, where you begin the neck shaping. Allow about 20cm width for the neck. Work out how many sts you need to have left on the shoulders: that is, width measurement minus 20cm, divided by two = shoulder measurement.

Shaping Round Neck

Leave sts for front of neck on a stitch-holder: about 14cm wide to start with (work out the number of stitches). Now working on one side at a time, decrease 1 st on alternate rows at neck edge until you have the number of sts for the shoulder. Work straight to match length of back. Work the other shoulder the same, matching the neck decreases.

Shoulders

Put sts of front shoulder parallel with back, wrong sides together, and using a third needle, cast off right through both sets of sts to make a ridge on the outside of the shoulder. Work the other shoulder the same, leaving sts for back of neck on a holder.

Sleeves

The sleeves are knitted from the armhole down towards the cuff. Work out how many sts you need for the top of the sleeve, which will measure twice the depth of the armhole. Using a shorter circular needle, pick up sts round the armhole, beginning at the bottom of the armhole, picking up half for the front, and half for the back.

To pick up the stitches evenly, you need markers at regular intervals round the armhole: if you have a stripe in the pattern, use this as a guide; or alternatively measure and mark the half-way and quarter points with safety pins, and divide up your stitches accordingly so that you pick up the same number between each marker.

Knit the sleeve in the round, working straight for 10cm, but marking the exact underarm point (where the seam would be) with a stitch marker, or a tag of yarn. Now measure how long the sleeve needs to be from here to above the cuff, and make these calculations: how many rows are there in this length, and how many stitches do you need above the cuff?

Subtract these stitches from the stitches at the top of the sleeve, and divide by 2, (as you will decrease 2 sts each time) = x.

Divide the number of rows by x, and this tells you how often to decrease. If the answer is something awkward like 4.2, you will have a few more stitches than you hoped for at the cuff. Decide if it is better to have more stitches or fewer stitches when you reach the cuff, and adjust accordingly with perhaps an occasional extra decrease.

Decrease your two stitches either side of the underarm marker, every few rows according to your calculation, moving onto four double-ended needles when the sleeve becomes too narrow for the circular needle.

Example: if your sleeve shaping is to be over a length of 30cm, and you are knitting a pattern with 28 rows = 10cm, there will be

$$\frac{30}{10} \times 28 = 84 \text{ rows for the sleeve shaping.}$$

If your sleeve top has 120 sts, and you would like to have 64 before you start the cuff, you need to decrease 56 sts. You will decrease 2 sts each time, so there will be 28 decreases. Now divide 84 rows by 28 decreases: = 3. Therefore decrease 2 sts underarm every 3rd row.

A very rough rule of thumb with sleeve shaping is to decrease every 4th row; this will apply if the jumper is plain, average-sized, and using stocking stitch. Other stitches that pull in or pull up more will have to be worked out as above.

Cuff

Knit the cuff in your chosen stitch, on appropriate needles, decreasing in the first row if necessary to make a narrower cuff, and cast off at the end.

Finishing the Neck

Using a short circular needle, or four double-ended, pick up sts from holder at back of neck, along side of neck, from holder at front of neck, and along side of neck, and knit in your chosen stitch, then cast off loosely. Tidy up the loose ends (woven in as the jumper was knitted) and now the jumper is finished.

SOME WAYS TO VARY THIS BASIC SHAPE

Jackets

Traditionally in some areas, jumpers and jackets have been worked in the round all the way through from the welt to the shoulders, with the armhole openings and front opening for a jacket cut at the end, and the raw edges bound. The reasoning behind this is that it may be easier to work in the round, particularly for stocking stitch, as you always work on the knit side with the pattern facing, and there is no need to purl. However, although this may be a speedy way to make a jacket, it is not always the most satisfactory way. When the technique of hand knitting can produce any shapes you want with ready-made selvedges, it seems to go against the nature of knitting to cut the fabric, and may make an unnecessarily clumsy edge.

In order to make a jacket following the guidelines given for the jumper above,

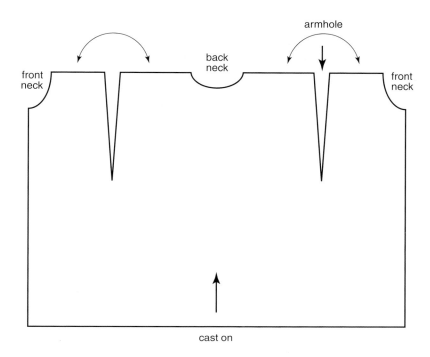

Spread of simple jacket shape, knitted in one piece.

instead of knitting in the round, the body is still knitted in one piece with no side seams, but travelling in rows backwards and forwards. A circular needle is still useful as it is long enough to carry the stitches comfortably, and spread out the whole width.

Body Variations

The body can be shaped by increasing and decreasing, or by using different stitches to pull in or spread out the fabric.

Armholes

With no armhole shaping, the sleeve will hang from a 'dropped shoulder'. In order to make a set-in sleeve, measure across the shoulders (on a person or ready-made garment), and calculate how many stitches are needed. Now subtract this number of stitches from the stitches for the back (that is, half the body), and divide by two. This tells you how many stitches to cast off for the armhole after you have separated the front and back. The stitches can be cast off at the armhole edge at the beginning of the next two rows to make straight set-in sleeves, or

ABOVE: *Armhole shapings.*   BELOW: *Neck shapings.*

can be decreased a few at a time over several rows for a more rounded armhole.

NB: if the sleeve is set in, it cannot be knitted in the round until it is long enough to fit the armhole cast-off, but must be knitted back and forth on a circular needle, which is necessary to travel round the curve of the top of the armhole.

Back of Neck

This was not shaped at all in the simple jumper guide, but can be shaped similarly to the front of the neck, starting 5cm from the top instead of 10cm.

Shoulders

The shoulders can be shaped or sloped by working 'short rows': divide the number of shoulder stitches by three or four, and turn and leave this number of stitches behind on the needle, at the shoulder edge on alternate rows, slipping the first stitch after the turn each time until all stitches are worked. Now put front and back shoulders together as above, and cast off through both to make a ridge.

This cast-off ridge is very strong, and makes a good supportive shoulder join. To make a more decorative feature of this cast off, it could be done using a contrast colour, or even a decorative cast off, such as picot cast off. However, if you do not want the ridge to be visible, it could be done with right sides together so that the ridge is on the inside. Alternatively, it could be grafted instead for an invisible join.

Sleeves

Having worked out how to calculate for the sleeve shaping, this could be varied for wider or narrower sleeves. If the top of the sleeve needs to be full, you could pick up the stitches round the armhole as usual, but increase in the following row to make a gathered effect round the armhole.

Setting sleeves into the straight armhole opening described means that they are at right angles to the body, which can cause some bulkiness under the arm. A more angled sleeve can be shaped by marking the centre of the sleeve where it joins the shoulder seam, and decreasing either side of this centre instead of under the arm. The sleeve slopes down at a natural angle, but still allows for plenty of movement.

Cuffs

The edges of a garment need to be strong and to look finished, whether they are stretchy or flat and firm. Knitted downwards in this way means cuffs are easy to adjust for length, and easy to repair.

Neck

Functionally, the neck has to be elastic enough to pass over the head: a decorative cast off such as picot cast off can be useful in giving a more flexible neck opening. Otherwise, necks can be as decorative or plain as wanted, high or low, polo, turtle, with collar or without.

Shoulder shapings, filling shoulder shape on a dipping-shaped jacket, with front and back cast-off tog.

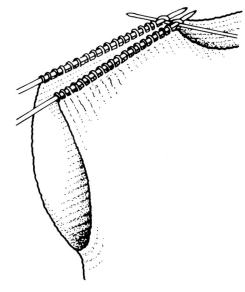

ABOVE: *Casting off shoulders.*

LEFT: *Picking up sts round front edges and neck to knit bands.*

6 PROJECTS

The projects begin with the simplest shaped jumper, knitted as shown in Chapter 5, all in one piece. Project 2 is another simple jumper, but knitted more unusually from the neck downwards; this makes it very easy to adjust the length. Again, it is knitted in the round, in one piece.

The next three projects are more complicated in shape, but intriguing to knit, covering knitting in different directions for each part (child's jacket, Project 3), 'bias' or 'chevron' knitting in the shaped waistcoat (Project 4), and knitting sideways to make the jacket (Project 5), which joins at the centre back.

The last two are for hats and cushions, with easy and more complicated variations, but all would lend themselves to experimenting with patterns and colours once the structure is understood.

OPPOSITE PAGE:
Detail of back of coat.

OPPOSITE PAGE:
Simple shaped
jumper.

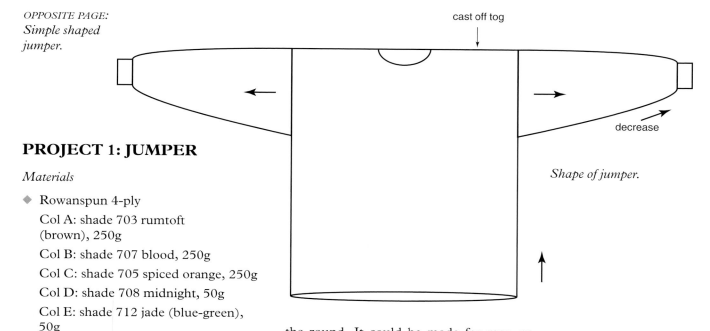

cast off tog

decrease

Shape of jumper.

PROJECT 1: JUMPER

Materials

◆ Rowanspun 4-ply

Col A: shade 703 rumtoft (brown), 250g

Col B: shade 707 blood, 250g

Col C: shade 705 spiced orange, 250g

Col D: shade 708 midnight, 50g

Col E: shade 712 jade (blue-green), 50g

Col F: shade 706 reed (dark green), 50g

◆ Circular needles size 3mm (11) and 3¼mm (10), 90 or 100cm length, + size 3mm (11) 40cm circular for neck, and if knitting sleeves in the round, 3¼mm (10) 40cm length, and 1 set of 4 double-ended needles in each size for sleeves and cuffs

◆ *Tension*: using needles 3¼mm (10) and knitting in pattern, 28 sts = 10cm

◆ *Size*: 102cm (40in), 108cm (42½in) or 115cm (45in) = actual measurement around chest/bust

Note: with 'reversible stretchy rib', it is correct for the 'wrong' colour to show in front of the purl stitches.

Description

This is a simple-shaped jumper, with straight body and tapered sleeves, knitted all in one piece, with body knitted in the round up to the armholes, shoulders cast off tog, and sleeves knitted downwards in the round. It could be made for men or women, in plain colour or stripes, or as illustrated in a 'Fair Isle' pattern with 2 colours per row (*see* diagram p.110).

Body

Using needles size 3mm (11), cast on 280 (300, 320) sts col A.

Work in reversible stretchy rib, cols A and C:

With right side facing, and *both yarns held at the back, K1 col A, then K1 col A weaving in C. Bring both yarns to the front, P1 col C, then P1 C, weaving in A.

Rep from * all round. Work straight in rib for 6cm (2½in).

K1 round, P1 round col A: the no of sts needs to be adjusted here in the middle size only so that the pattern fits exactly, so in this case increase evenly from 300 to 304 sts.

Now change to needles size 3¼mm (10) and begin pattern from chart (*see* p.110).

Work straight until it measures 40 (42, 44)cm 15½, (16½, 17½)in from beg.

Divide for armholes: leave half the sts on a spare circular needle for front, and work on back: 140 (152, 160) sts (*see* overleaf).

Back

*Cont in pattern, working backwards and forwards without shaping until it measures 23 (24, 25)cm 9 (9½, 10)in from armhole.

Back Neck Shaping

Put the centre 32 sts on a st holder, and working on one side at a time, continuing pattern, decrease 1 st at neck edge on alt rows until there are 56 sts left. Work straight until it measures 26 (27, 28)cm 10¼ (10½, 11)in from beg of armhole.

Put shoulder sts on holder, and work the other side to match.

Front

Work the same as back from *, until it measures 16 (17, 18)cm 6½ (6¾, 7)in from armhole.

Put the centre 28 sts on a holder, and, working on one side at a time, continuing pattern, decrease 1 st at neck edge on alt rows until there are 56 sts left. Work straight until the same length as back, then join shoulders.

Shoulders

With right side facing, K1 row col A across 56 shoulder sts of front, then without breaking wool, knit across 56 sts of corresponding back shoulder.

Pattern chart.

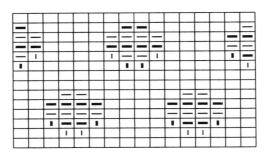

repeat

A   D

C   F

B   E

C   D

A   E

B   F

A   D

B   F

C   E

B   D

A   F

C   E

start here

RIGHT: Colour chart.

FAR RIGHT: Construction of back and front.

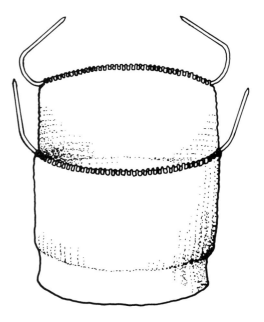

Putting back and front together, wrong sides tog, with sts parallel, use a crochet hook or 3rd needle to cast off through both together, making a ridge on the outside, col A.

Finish the other shoulder to match.

Sleeves

Using needles size 3¼mm (10) and col A, starting at bottom of armhole, pick up and knit 73 (76, 79) sts up one side to shoulder join and 73 (76, 79) sts down the other.

To pick up sts evenly, see how many pattern repeats there are along the armhole edge, and divide the no of sts by this; for example, if you need to pick up 76 sts and there are 14 stripes or repeats of the pattern, you need to pick up 5.5 sts to each repeat: perhaps 5 sts for one stripe, and 6 for the next.

Purl 1 round col A, then begin pattern.

Knitting in the round, work straight in pattern for 10cm (4in).

Mark the underarm 'seam' point, and decrease 1 st either side of this marker every 4th round until the sleeve measures 40 (42, 44)cm, 15½(16½, 17)in, changing to double-ended needles when sleeve becomes too narrow for circular needle.

Now K1 round, P1 round col A, decreasing evenly to 64 sts.

Change to needles size 3mm (11).

Cuff

Work in same rib as for welt for 5cm (2in), and cast off in rib col A.

Neck

Using needles size 3mm (11), starting at shoulder join, pick up 12 sts along side of back neck shaping, 32 sts from back neck stitch holders, 12 sts up other side of back of neck, 30 sts along side of neck, 28 sts from front neck holder, and 30 sts along other side of neck.

P1 round, then rib as for welt for 2½cm (1in), casting off in rib col A.

Alternative pattern, Project 1.

Variations

◆ Ribbing at welt cuffs and neck can be plain colour K1, P1, or K2, P2; or 2-colour stripy rib, knitting 2 sts col A and purling 2 col C, but always holding the yarns at the back. This rib will lie flat, and not be stretchy.

◆ Body pattern can be plain colour stocking st, or stripes of plain colours as shown above, or any Fair Isle pattern divisible by 8.

◆ Sleeves can be knitted with an underarm seam, which saves working on small circular or double-ended needles.

PROJECT 2:
SQUARE-YOKED JUMPER

Materials

◆ Rowan wool/cotton

Col A: shade 904 moonshine (grey), 700g, 800g

Col B: shade 947 spark (paprika red), 50g

◆ Needles, circular size 3¾mm (9), 90cm, and 40cm for the neck

◆ *Tension*: 22sts = 10cm

◆ *Size*: 117cm (46in), 122cm (48in), 128cm (50in)

Description

This is a square, loose-fitting boxy jumper. It is very simple to knit, worked from the neck downwards, increasing at 4 'corners' to make raglan shaping.

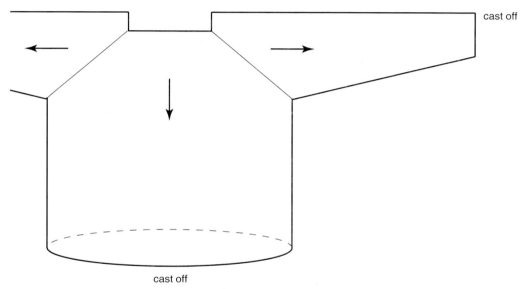

LEFT: Square-yoked jumper.

ABOVE: Shape of jumper.

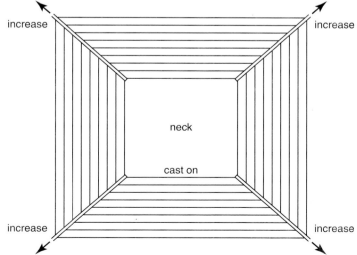

Beginning from the neck.

Constructing the yoke to the armholes.

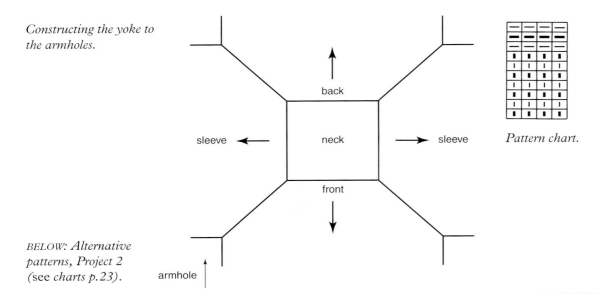

Pattern chart.

BELOW: *Alternative patterns, Project 2 (see charts p.23).*

Neck and Yoke

Cast on 120 (128, 128) sts col B on the small circular needle.

Change to col A, K1 round, P3 rounds. Now begin increasing:

mark with tags of yarn or stitch markers at the 4 increasing points:

36 (38, 38) sts for front and back, and 24 (26, 26) for sleeves. So: 36 (38, 38) sts, marker, 24 (26, 26) sts, marker, 36 (38, 38) sts, marker, 24 (26, 26) sts.

Round 1) * K1, O, K34 (36, 36), O, K1, (marker), K1, O, K22 (24, 24), O, K1, (marker) * rep from * to *.

The marker will always be in the centre of 2 knit sts with incs on either side of them.

Round 2) knit all round.

Round 3) increase again: * K1, O, K36 (38, 38), O, K1, (marker), K1, O, K24 (26, 26), O, K1, (marker) * rep from * to *.

Round 4) knit.

Cont in this way, until round 7 is completed, increasing on alt rounds, keeping markers in place so incs make a neat line, and there will be 2 more sts between incs each time, with 2 sts always at the corners.

Rounds 8, 9, and 10, purl all round without increasing, *but still knit the 2 sts between the incs.*

These 10 rows form the pattern.

Cont in this manner until there are 456 (480, 496) sts: (120, 126, 130) sts for front and back, and 108 (114, 116) for each sleeve.

Body

Now put sleeve sts on stitch holders or spare circular needles, 108 (114, 116) for each, and work on main body, working in the round, and continuing the same pattern with ridges.

Cast on 4 sts, then knit across the 120 (126, 130) sts of the front, cast on 8 sts, knit 120 (126, 130) sts, cast on 4.

256 (268, 276)sts.

Knitting in the round, cont in pattern until it measures 30 (32, 34) cm from armhole, and finish on a 'ridge', then cast off col B.

Sleeves

You will need a circular needle because of the shape at the top of the sleeve, but it can be knitted either in the round, or back and forth with an underarm seam sewn at the end. If knitted in the round, it will be necessary to go on to 4 double-ended needles as the sleeve decreases.

The instructions are written for knitting back and forth: if you knit round, mark the underarm decreasing point to keep the decs straight.

The pattern for knitting back and forth changes to:

Row 1) knit, row 2) purl, row 3) knit, row 4) purl, row 5) knit, row 6) purl, row 7) knit (this makes the 7 rows stocking st).

Row 8) knit, row 9) purl, row 10) knit (this makes the reverse st st ridge).

Row 1) cast on 4, pattern 108 (114, 116) cast on 4.

Now continue in pattern as before, decreasing 1 st at each end of every 4th row, thus: K1, S1, K1, psso, work to last 2 sts, K2 tog.

When sleeve measures 40cm from armhole, cast off col B to match body.

Sew sleeve seam, fasten off ends.

Variations

◆ Edges could be ribbed for a closer fitting welt and cuffs.

◆ The shape of this jumper could be transformed into a simple, slim-fitting jumper if it was worked in K2, P2 rib throughout.

◆ Knit in a textured st, such as knit and purl squares

◆ Edges could be cast on and off in a decorative st, for example picot.

PROJECT 3:
CHILD'S JACKET

Materials

◆ Jaeger Baby merino 4-ply

   Col A: shade 108 airforce
   (darker grey), 100g (150g)

   Col B: shade 107 cuddle
   (lighter grey), 100g

Col C: shade 105 mousse (light pink),
100g

Col D: shade 119 cranberry
(deep pink), 100g

Col E: shade 106 stone (natural), 50g

◆ Needles size 3¼mm (10) and 3mm
   (11), straight or circular

◆ *Tension*:
   Yoke and sleeve pattern: 27 sts = 10cm
   Main pattern: 30 sts = 10cm

OPPOSITE PAGE:
Child's jacket.

ABOVE: Back of jacket.

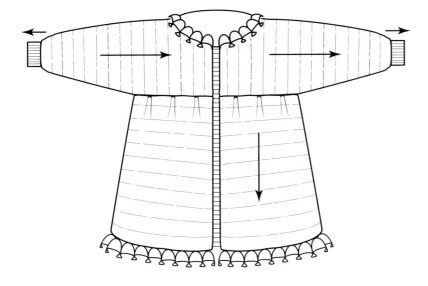

Yoke and Sleeves

The sleeve is cast on above the cuff, and the cuffs knitted last, so that they can be added to for growth.

Cast on 50 (60) sts col A, using a method of casting on that will be easy to pick up later to knit the cuff, such as provisional cast on, or knit-on cast on. Begin pattern (*see* p.120 for chart):

Row 1) col A, knit
Row 2) col A, knit
Row 3) col A, purl
Row 4) col A, knit
Row 5) change to col D, knit
Row 6) col D, purl.

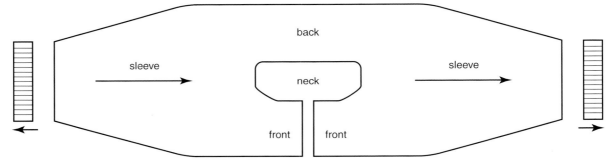

TOP: Shape and directions of knitting.

Yoke and sleeves.

◆ *Size*: actual measurement: chest 80cm (31in), (88cm (34½in))
Length: 42cm (16½in) (50cm (20in))

To fit approximately 2 yr old (4 yr old)

Description
This jacket is designed for growth, so that the sleeve or body length can be added to later. The yoke is knitted first, using a stretchy welting stitch for expansion, worked sideways from cuff to cuff, and both cuffs are knitted with a cast-off edge. Stitches are picked up along the bottom of the yoke and the body is knitted downwards, ending in a frill. Neck and front bands are knitted last.

Rep these 6 rows, increasing 1 st at each end of every 4th row until there are 82 (92 sts), in colour sequence:
Rows 1–4 alternating A and B, rows 5 and 6 in D, C and E in this order.

Work straight in this pattern until the sleeve measures 38 (44)cm. (NB this is not the length of the arm, but the length to the neck shaping).

Neck Shaping

With right side facing, pattern 36 (41) sts (these sts will be the front, and can be put on a stitch holder), cast off 10 for the neck, and pattern to end. Working on these last 36 (41) sts for the back, decrease 1 st at neck edge (at beginning of right-side rows) every

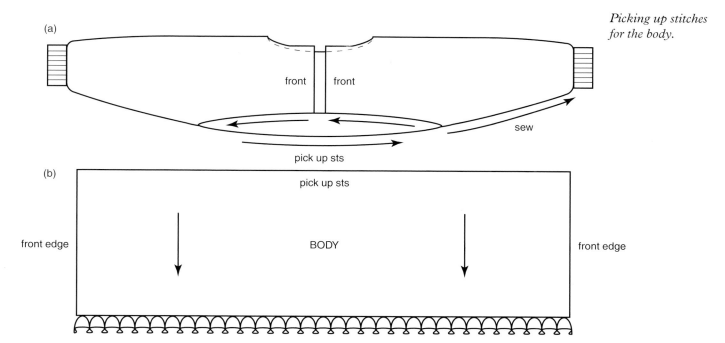

4th row until there are 31 (36) sts. Work straight in pattern until you are 10cm from beg of neck (don't stretch out too much), then cast on 1 st at neck edge every 4th row until you have 36 (41) sts again. The neck needs to measure 15cm across.

Hold these sts, and go back to the sts for front of neck. Work in the same way, continuing in pattern and casting off 1 st at neck edge until there are 24 (29) sts.

Now work straight until it measures 7½cm from beg of neck shaping (or halfway along back neck shaping): this will be the front opening. Put sts on a holder, and break off yarn. Now for second half of neck, cast on 24 (29) sts (again using a cast-on that can be picked up later) and work to match first half, working straight for the same distance, then casting on 1 st at neck edge every 4th row until there are 36 (41) sts.

This should now be the same length as the back, and you can work all across 82 (92) sts again, and make the second sleeve.

Fold the knitting in half to measure how far to work until you reach the sleeve shaping, then decrease 1 st at each end of next and every 4th row until there are 50 (60) sts again.

Cuff

Work in K2, P2 reversible stretchy rib using 1 col for knit, and the other for purl. This is a strong and decorative rib, worked in 2 colours: *see below* for variations. It will show a different colour on the cuffs if they are turned back.

2-Colour Reversible Stretchy Rib

Row 1) using cols A and D, *hold both yarns to the back, and K1 col A, K1 col A weaving in col D. Bring both yarns to the front, and P1 col D, P1 col D, weaving in col A.

Repeat from * to end of row.
Row 2) working in K2, P2 rib with the same colours on the same sts as in the previous row, *hold both yarns to the back, and K1 col D, K1 col D weaving in col A. Bring both yarns to the front, and P1 col A, P1 col A, weaving in col D. Repeat from * to end of row.

skirt pattern

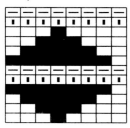

yoke and sleeves pattern

Pattern charts.

FAR RIGHT: Colour chart.

Work a 3cm cuff, and cast off in rib in col A.

For the 2nd cuff, pick up the original cast-on sts, and work another cuff to match.

Body

Sew underarm seam for sleeves, measuring 29cm (11½in), 34cm (13½in) length for each sleeve, including cuff.

The sts for the body are now picked up, starting at front opening, with right side facing (*see* p.119). Using col A, pick up 60 (66) sts along front edge, 121 (133) across back, and 60 (66) sts for 2nd front. It might help to pick up the stitches evenly if you divide the no of sts by the no of ridges, to work out how many sts to pick up to each ridge of pattern (total sts = 241 (265) sts).

Knit back col A, then begin pattern from chart, which will fit exactly with 1 extra st so front edges match.

Work in pattern for 23 (31)cm.

Frilled Edge

Knit 2 rows col A, increasing evenly to 245 (269) sts, then begin frill with right side facing.

Row 1) knit col D
Row 2) * K5, P1 * rep to last 5 sts, K5
Row 3) * P5 M1, K1, M1*, ending P5
Row 4) * K5, P3 *, ending K5
Row 5) change to col C, * P5, K3 *, ending P5
Row 6) as row 4
Row 7) increase again: * P5, M1, K3, M1 *, ending P5
Row 8) *K5, P5 *, ending K5
Row 9) change to col D, *P5, K5 *, ending P5
Row 10) as row 8.

Cont in this way, working in stripes of 4 rows each of D and C, increasing either side of the K sts every 4th row until you have K9, P5, and complete the 4-row stripe.

Cast off in col A, still in knit and purl.

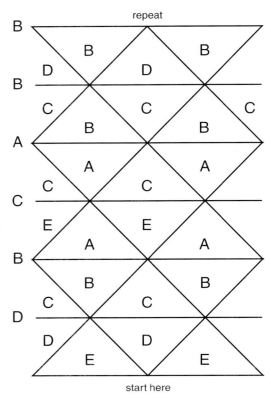

Neck

Using needles size 3mm (11) and col A, pick up and knit 26 sts along right front, 53 sts along back of neck, and 26 sts along other front, not including front bands.

Frilled Neck

This frill starts from the widest part, decreasing to make the 'bell' shapes: the opposite to the frill at the bottom, which increases outwards to the edge.

Row 2) col A: * K5, cast on 9* rep, ending K5.

The cast on sts can be either *single thumb twist cast on*, which works in the same direction as the knitting, is very neat, but difficult to knit in the following row; or *cable cast on* where you will need to turn the work at each cast on, then turn back again to knit (*see* 'Casting on', Chapter 3).

Row 3) change to col D, knit

Row 4) ★ K5, P9 ★ rep to end of row, ending K5

Row 5) ★ P5, K2 tog, K5, S1, K1, psso★ rep, ending P5

Row 6) ★ K5, P7 ★ rep to end of row, ending K5

Row 7) col C: ★ P5, K2 tog, K3, S1, K1, psso ★ rep, ending P5

Row 8) ★ K5, P5 ★ rep to end of row, ending K5

Row 9) ★ P5, K2 tog, K1, S1, K1, psso ★ rep, ending P5

Row 10) ★ K5, P3 ★ rep to end of row, ending K5

Row 11) col D: ★ P5, S1, K2 tog, psso ★ rep, ending P5

Row 12) ★ K5, P1 ★ rep to end of row, ending K5

Row 13) ★ P4, K2 tog ★, rep to end of row, ending P5

Row 14) using col A, cast off.

Front Bands

Using needles size 3mm (11) and col A, pick up and knit sts along front edge, including yoke and frill. Pick up 5 sts to each pattern repeat, as in illustration, or adjust to fit your tension.

The stitches held at front of yoke need to be increased slightly, as the ribbing will pull in more than the welting stitch of the yoke. Increase 1 st every 10 sts across yoke.

Work in reversible stretchy rib as described above, for 6 rows. Cast off in rib col A.

Buttonholes may be made at intervals on one front band.

Buttonholes

This is a strong buttonhole, completed in 1 row. Work to the chosen position for buttonhole. Bring yarn to the front of work, and drop it.

★ Slip another st from LH needle to RH needle, pass 1st slip st over 2nd to cast off 1st st. Rep from ★ until required no of sts are cast off.

Slip last cast-off st back onto LH needle.

Turn work.

Pick up the hanging yarn and pass it between needles to the back. Using cable cast on, cast on 1 more st than you cast off, but do not place last st on LH needle yet. Bring yarn back through to the front between last 2 sts, put last st on needle. Turn work.

Slip end st from LH needle to RH needle, then cast off extra cast on st over it. Work to next buttonhole position and repeat process.

Sew in loose ends, sew on buttons.

Variations

◆ For a simpler version, the main pattern could be moss stitch stripes (*right*), working 2 rows of each colour. NB Following the given instructions, this stitch would make a wider, fuller coat than the 'Fair Isle' pattern illustrated.

◆ All ribbing could be single coloured K2, P2 rib, instead of 2-coloured.

◆ Instead of frills at neck and bottom edge, a plainer version or a boy's jacket could have ribbed edges.

◆ Another alternative edge for the bottom of the jacket could be a small reverse stocking stitch roll, or plain garter stitch, which could easily be undone and more length added to the main pattern when needed.

Alternative pattern, Project 3: moss st stripes.

PROJECT 4: WAISTCOAT

Materials

◆ Circular needles size 3¼mm (10) and 3mm (11) (straight needles could be used for the body, but the length of a circular needle is useful for spreading out the full width).

◆ Jaeger Matchmaker Merino 4-ply

Col A: shade 698 indigo (dark blue), 200g

Col B: shade 722 iris (bright blue), 150g

Col C: shade 726 spice (paprika red), 50g

Col D: shade 639 granite (grey), 50g
Col E: shade 725 lagoon (light greeny blue), 50g

OPPOSITE PAGE: Waistcoat.

ABOVE: Waistcoat back.

Whole shape spread.

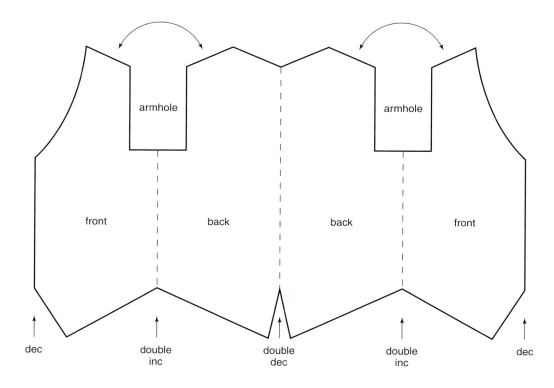

- ◆ *Tension*: 30 sts = 10cm over pattern

- ◆ *Size*: actual measurement at bust: 92cm (36in), 100cm (39½in), 107cm, (42in)

Description

This waistcoat is knitted in the 'Fair Isle' way with 2 colours in a row, weaving in the second colour. All loose ends can be woven in the same way, and snipped off. The shape is begun in 2 pieces from centre front to centre back. These are joined above the back vent, and the waistcoat is then made all in one piece, with decreases at front edges and centre back, and increases at the sides that cause the shape to dip slightly down at the front and back and up at the sides. The armhole bands and front edge, and edgings for back vent and underarm are knitted last.

Facing for Bottom Edge

Using needles size 3mm (11), cast on 126 (138, 150) sts col A, work 8 rows stocking st for the facing. (This will turn under and be stitched in place, and prevent the bottom edge from curling up.)

Pattern chart.

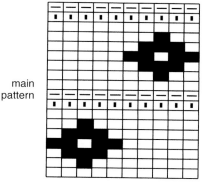

main pattern

border pattern

124

End facing on a purl row, then beginning with a purl row, work 4 rows reverse stocking st in the same colour (purl side is right side):
Row 1) purl
Row 2) knit
Row 3) purl
Row 4) knit
Change to needle size 3¼mm (10), and begin pattern from chart, beginning with Border Pattern cols D and E and increasing in the first row every 12th st to make 138 (150, 162) sts. The border ends with a knit-2-rows ridge col A.

Now begin shaping at sides, and Main Pattern from chart.
Row 1) pattern 69 (75, 81) pick up and knit 2 strands before next st (making 2 new sts): this = side seam point: pattern 69 (75, 81) sts.
The pattern needs to 'mirror image' at the side point. To do this, work to the side point, increase, then place the next motif the same distance from the increase as the last one was.
Row 2) pattern in purl
Row 3) pattern in K
Row 4) pattern in P
Then rep from row 1 increasing in the middle of the row. The next inc row will be pattern 70 (76, 82) sts, inc 2, pattern 70 (76, 82) sts.

Cont shaping every 4th row, marking the increasing point at the centre of the row, as increases must be exactly above each other.

The gap between the motifs at the side point will widen, and the no of sts increase, until there is room to begin a new motif in the gap.

Work until it measures 10cm from beg of pattern. There should now be 150 (162, 174) sts.

Put this piece on a stitch holder or spare circular needle, and work another piece exactly the same, making sure that the motifs are the same distance from the edge that will become centre back as on the first

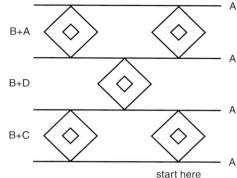

Colour chart.

piece, that is, the right-hand edge of the first piece must mirror the left-hand edge of second piece.

Join Together
With the right side facing, pattern all across 300 (324, 348 sts), work 1 row back in pattern in purl.

From now on the following shaping will continue throughout the waistcoat:

Dec 1 st at front edges, double inc at 'side seam' (as before), and also double dec at centre back every 4th row in this way:

Right side facing, K2 tog, work in pattern to side marker and increase either side of marker as before, work in pattern to 2 sts before centre back: S1, K1, psso, (centre marker) K2 tog: pattern to side marker, increasing as before, and pattern to last 2 sts: S1, K1, psso.

The no of sts will now stay the same, and the pattern will converge at centre back, and grow outwards from the sides. It is essential to keep the incs and decs in line, and to keep the motifs spaced evenly.

Armholes
When it measures 30 (32, 34)cm, from beg of pattern, divide for armholes.

Put 75 (81, 87) sts of each front on holders, and work on 150 (162, 174) sts for back.

Back

Cont in pattern, cast off 10 (11, 11) sts at beg of every row until there are 90 (96, 108) sts left, meanwhile still doing double dec centre back every 4th row. Now work straight, cont dec at centre back, and also inc 1 st at each armhole edge every 4th row, so number of sts remains constant. When it measures 26cm from armhole, hold sts.

Fronts

Cast off 10 (11, 11) sts at armhole edge on alt rows, until there are 45 (48, 54) sts, meanwhile cont in pattern, then inc 1 st at armhole edge every 4th row for the rest of the front, but also begin neck shaping:

Dec 1 st on ALT rows at front edge.
Cont until 24 sts left. Now cont on these sts, inc and dec as before every 4th row, until it measures same as back.

Shoulder Shaping

Right Front
pattern across, turn
   2) purl
   3) pattern to last 3 sts, turn
   4) purl
Cont leaving 3 more sts behind each K row, ending with a P row. Work 2 more rows all across, then using col A, K across. Without breaking thread, K across 24 sts of corresponding back shoulder, then put front and back parallel, wrong sides tog, and cast off both tog using a 3rd needle or crochet hook, col A. (This makes a ridge on the outside – similar to shoulder shaping on p.105.)

Left Front
Work to match right front, then when you reach the shoulder, pattern all across, turn.
   2) P to last 3 sts, turn
   3) K (pattern)
   4) P, as before, leaving 3 more sts. Cont, ending with a K row, then P1 row, K and P 2 more rows (always in pattern), and work shoulder join as on 1st shoulder.

Armhole Bands

Although these are worked back and forth, a circular needle is needed as it makes it possible to work over the curve of the shoulder.

Using col A, pick up and K about 156 sts round armhole, 78 up front, and 78 down back, but not underarm, which is stitched down at the end.

To work this out accurately, check how many sts you have to 10cm, measuring across the pattern somewhere on the waist-coat.

Divide depth of armhole (26cm) by 10cm, and multiply by no of sts in 10cm.

That is, if 30 sts = 10cm, $2.6 \times 30 = 78$, with a calculator this is straightforward.

If your tension is different, adjust the no of sts: it is critical that the armhole band sits well.

To make sure the top of the armband lies flat, pick sts up more sparingly over top of shoulder.

K back 1 row.

Work border pattern from chart, in cols D and E, finishing with the 'ridge', (K 2 rows col A). Now change to needle size 3mm (11) and knit in reversible stretchy rib cols A and B.

Right side: * with both yarns held at the back, K1 A, K1 A weaving in B. Bringing both yarns forward, P1 B, P1 B weaving in A. Rep from * to end of rib.

Wrong-side rows; keeping same cols on same sts, * K1 col B, K1 B weaving A, yarns forward, P1 A, P1 A weaving B. Rep from * to end of rib.

Work for 2½cm (1in), and cast off col A in rib.

The 'wrong' colour shows on the purl stitches, but it makes a good strong, stretchy, stripy rib.

Stitch the armhole band to the underarm, then work the underarm edging (*see* p.127, top left).

Underarm

Using needles size 3mm (11), pick up and knit sts along underarm edge from the

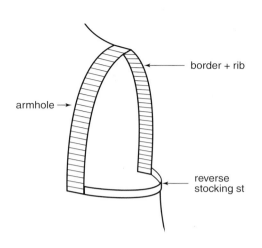

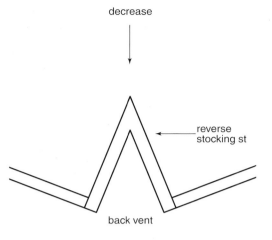

cast-off sts, col A. Beginning on next row with a knit row, work in reverse stocking st for 5 rows and cast off.

Back Vent

Using needles size 3mm (11), pick up sts along edge of back vent col A, picking up 3 sts every 4 rows. Work in reverse stocking st, as for underarm edge, and at centre back, dec 2 sts *every row*. The neatest way to do this is K3 tog on knit rows, P3 tog on purl rows. Work 6 rows and cast off.

Front Bands

Needles size 3mm (11). Work in reverse stocking st for the bottom of front edges to match back vent (*see* diagram, above right), but for the rest in reversible stretchy rib.

With right side facing, pick up sts from bottom of front edge all the way up the front (more generously over the curve of the front shaping), round the neck, down the other front to the bottom. Knit back 1 row.

Right-side rows: purl to beg of rib col A, then begin ribbing:

yarns back, K1 A, K1 A weaving in B. Yarns both forward, P1 B, P1 B weaving in A. Rep to end of rib, then P to end col A.

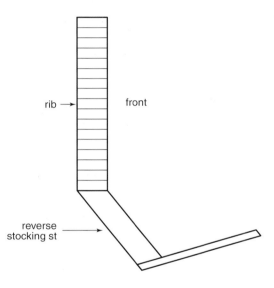

Front edge details.

Wrong-side rows; K to beg of rib col A, then keeping same cols on same sts, K1 col B, K1 B weaving A, yarns forward, P A, P1 A weaving in B. Rep to end of rib. K col A to end. Rib for 5 rows, cast off col A.

Sew in loose ends, turn bottom facing under and stitch, and if you want buttons, attach buttons and crochet loops.

PROJECT 5: JACKET WITH SHAPED BACK

Materials

◆ Circular needles size 4mm (8)

◆ Rowan Magpie Aran yarn
  Col A: shade 625 charcoal, 800g

Col B: shade 318 misty (light grey), 300g

Col C: shade 320 truffle (brown), 300g

Col D: magpie tweed shade 779 rumble (dark grey), 200g

◆ *Tension*: 18–20 sts = 10cm over Fair Isle.

◆ *Size*: loose fit, one size: the looser the tension, the larger the jacket.

OPPOSITE PAGE:
Jacket with shaped back.

ABOVE: Back of jacket.

Construction of knitting for jacket: a) left piece, b) right piece.

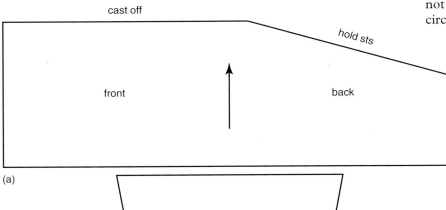

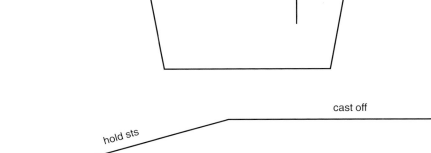

(a)

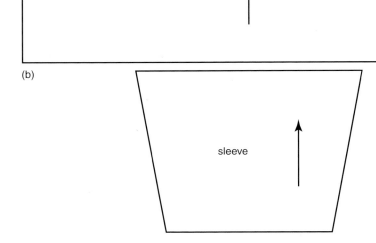

(b)

Description

This jacket is knitted across the garment, not in the round, but back and forth. The circular needles are useful as there are a lot of stitches. It is made in 4 pieces: the body is knitted as half back and front in one piece, and sleeves either separately, or they could be knitted onto the body making 2 pieces, but this would make the knitting quite heavy.

The jacket is shaped along the centre back seam, which is joined at the end, and the fronts also slope and may overlap at the bottom edge.

Sleeve

Starting with the cuff, cast on 64 sts col A, and work in garter st (every row knit) for 8 rows.

Now begin main pattern from chart, increasing 1 st at each end of next and every 2nd row until there are 86 sts, then at each end of every 4th row until there are 110 sts.

Work straight until it measures 30cm, finishing with 4 rows garter st col A.

Cast off, but don't fasten off thread, as this can be used to graft the stitches to the body. Work 2.

Body

If you want to knit the body joined on to the sleeve, cast on 95 sts at beg of next 2 rows (= 300 sts altogether) or:

Starting at sideseam edge, cast on 300 sts. Work in pattern for 26cm, then start back shaping.

Right Front and Back

Every right-side row, leave the last 5 sts at the end of the row on the needle, turn and pattern back. Leave 5 more sts behind on alt rows until 140 sts are being held, and the 160 sts left are being worked.

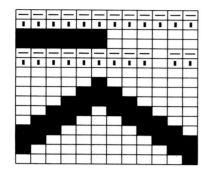

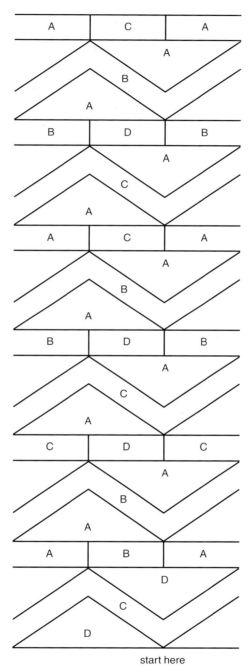

FAR LEFT: *Pattern chart.*

LEFT: *Colour chart.*

This should now measure between 40 and 50cm.

Leave this half on a thread or spare circular needle, and work:

Left Front and Back

in the same way, but for the back shaping, leave the sts at the end of wrong-side rows (*see* diagram p.130).

To Join Back

Leave the sts for the front on holders (160 sts each front), and using col A, begin at bottom of left back with right side facing, knit along all the held sts, knitting an extra st at each 'step' (where you turned to knit back), picking up the st from the row below.

Without breaking the yarn, knit down the sts for right back in the same way, finishing at bottom of right back.

To join: to make a strong ridge along the centre back, put both backs parallel with wrong sides tog, and cast off through both sets of sts (a crochet hook makes this easier) (*see* p.39).

Joining Sides and Sleeves

Sew the sleeve and side seams, or crochet the sides to match centre back.

Bottom Welts

The welts are knitted separately for fronts and back, leaving the sides open.

Back: with right side facing, pick up stitches from bottom edge of back col A.

start here

To work out exactly how many sts to pick up, measure across the bottom edge, then put the tape measure across the knitting to

Alternative pattern and chart for project 5.

see how many sts you have to this measurement. If your tension is different for garter st, measure the tension in the cuffs as a guide.

Knit in garter st for 10 rows, and cast off. Make the front welts in the same way.

Front and Neck Bands

Beginning at bottom of right front welt, right side facing, knit up sts from holder using col A. Work all the way round the fronts and neck, using 2 circular needles for extra length. Work in garter st for 10 rows.

Try the jacket on to see where you need buttonholes, and mark the positions with safety pins. Depending on the fit, the fronts may slope and overlap, and you may only want one or two buttons in the front. Make buttonholes on right band on the 7th row, and cast off after 10 rows.

Variations

◆ Instead of the charted pattern, this jacket could be knitted in moss st with slip-st stripes, as in the sample illustrated, or it could be plain stocking st or garter st stripes.

◆ Alternative edgings: instead of garter st, use ribbing; but in this case, you may need extra sts for the front bands, as the sts held for the front bands will be pulled in by ribbing. Try increasing 1 st every 12th st as you begin the rib.

PROJECT 6: HATS

Materials

◆ Circular needle 50cm or shorter and 4
double-ended needles size 3¾mm (9)

◆ Any double knitting yarn: the hats
illustrated are knitted in a cotton yarn
and a silk

◆ *Tension*: 21 sts = 10cm over pattern

◆ *Size*: to fit head size 56cm (22in).

Round hat.

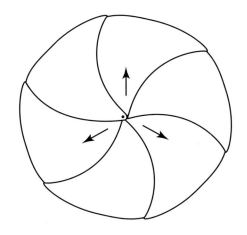 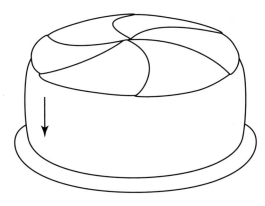

Charts for round hat.

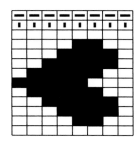

Round Hat

Description
Knitted without seams from the top of the hat on double-ended needles, going onto a circular needle, casting off at bottom edge.

Cast on 6 sts onto one double-ended needle
Round 1) using 2nd needle, ★ O, K1, O, K1 ★
 3rd needle, rep ★ to ★
 4th needle, rep ★ to ★
Round 2) joining into a circle, knit all round
Round 3) change colour, and on each needle, O, K2, O, K2
Round 4) purl all round
 Rep these 4 rows, increasing at beg and middle of each needle on odd rounds:
 1) increase round, 2) knit round, 3) increase round, 4) purl round.
 Work in 2 rounds of each colour.
 Change to circular needle when there are enough stitches.
 Continue until there are 120 sts.
 Finish on Row 4: if necessary, K 1 round, P 1 round to finish on a 'ridge'.
 Now follow chart and knit straight sides of hat until the pattern is complete.
 Hat edge: using main colour, K 1 round. Now work 5 rounds purl, decreasing 6 sts evenly on the first round. Cast off and sew in end.

Pointed Hat

Materials

◆ as for round hat.

Description
This hat is knitted the other way up, starting at the bottom.

Size: to fit head sizes 53 (56, 58)cm, 21 (22, 23) in

Using the circular needle, cast on 108 (114, 120) sts, and knit stocking st for 5cm. This will give a rolled edge that can be stitched later, or padded and stitched to make a bigger roll.
 On the last row, increase evenly to 114 (120, 126) sts.

Pointed hat.

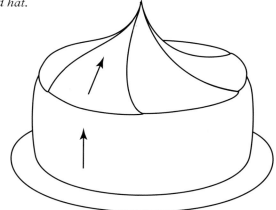

Hat crown for both hats

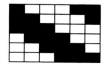

Chart for pointed hat.

Now begin pattern from chart, and work straight until as deep as you want it.

Crown

K1 round, P1 round.

Now start decreasing: ＊ K17 (18, 19), K2 tog ＊, rep all round

Working in this pattern:

1) decrease round, 2) knit round, 3) decrease round, 4) purl round.

Work in 2 rounds of each colour.

The next decrease round will be ＊K16 (17, 18), K2 tog＊, and the next 1 st less.

When the circular needle becomes uncomfortable as the sts decrease, change to double-ended needles.

Work until you have 2 sts left per needle.

Knit round, then K2 tog all round. Cast the last 3 sts off, leaving 1 st: by using a crochet hook and working a few sts of chain the point can be extended if you want: then fasten off.

PROJECT 7: CUSHIONS

Materials

◆ Needles size 4mm (8); circular are needed for cushion B, and for all finishing.

◆ Rug yarn or similar weight yarn, a selection of greys and blacks.

This yarn and pattern will make a good tough floor cushion measuring 66cm (26in) square.

◆ *Tension*: 18 sts = 10cm

Cushion A

Description

This cushion is worked in 4 triangles, each one picked up from the side of the previous one, and knitted in a different direction. The illustration (*below*) shows a smaller cushion being constructed in the same way.

Triangle 1) using col A, cast on 88 sts. K2 rows col A.

Begin 'squares' pattern from chart, and at the end of each right-side row, leave the last st, and turn and work back; leaving one more st behind each right-side row.

As there are 5 rows to each square, leaving 1 st at end of each right-side row will

OPPOSITE PAGE:
Cushion A.

Construction of cushion A (different patterns).

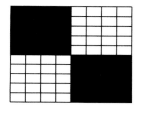 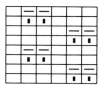 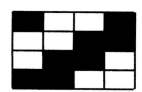

LEFT: Border for cushion B.

Pattern for cushions A and B   *Pattern for cushion A*

only have left 3 sts, and a whole square (that is, 4 sts) needs to be left by the end of 5 rows. So once during each square, leave 2 sts behind. This makes a neat diagonal edge across the squares pattern.

The colours are varied by changing 1 or both in each row of squares.

Work until the last st of the last square is being worked.

Hold all the held sts on thread (you need to be able to stretch the triangle out to its full size), and begin next triangle.

Pick up and knit 88 sts evenly along straight right-hand edge of previous triangle. K 3 rows, then work as for 1st triangle but work in spot pattern (*see* chart, above middle), leaving sts held at ends of right-side rows as before.

The colours are changed every 2, 4 or 6 rows.

Triangle 3 is 'squares' pattern, and triangle 4 is spots.

When 4 triangles are completed, sew the side of triangle 4 to the cast-on edge of triangle 1.

Make 2 sides for the cushion.

To join: knit sts held on threads around edge of the piece, increasing evenly to make 5 or 6 sts out of every 4 sts held. This is the longest edge of the triangle, therefore you need more sts than were cast on for the straight edge.

When you have knitted round the edges of both pieces, put the 2 sides wrong sides tog, and cast off through both sets of sts, to make a firm ridge around the edge.

To leave an opening, cast off some or all of the last edges separately, and hand sew in a zip or other fastening.

Cushion B

Cast on 112 sts col A, and work in squares pattern (*see* chart, above left) until the piece is as long as it is wide, to the nearest complete pattern. Depending on your tension, there may be the same no of squares in both directions.

Using a long circular needle, pick up sts all round the edge of the cushion, the same no for each edge, and knit a border in diagonal pattern (*see* chart above right), increasing 2 sts at each corner on alt rows, until it is the size you want.

Hold the edge sts, so it can be finished as for cushion 1.

BIBLIOGRAPHY

BOOKS ON TECHNIQUE, STITCHES AND PATTERNS

These are not all in print, but are well worth searching for:

Ellen, Alison, *The Handknitter's Design Book* (David & Charles, 1992).
Harmony Guides to Knitting Stitches (4 paperback vols) (Lyric Books).
Lorant, Tessa, *Knitted Quilts and Flounces* (Thorn Press, 1982).
Stanley, Montse, *The Handknitter's Handbook* (David and Charles, 1986).
Mary Thomas's Knitting Book (Hodder and Stoughton, 1938).
Mary Thomas's Book of Knitting Patterns (Hodder and Stoughton, 1943).
Walker, Barbara, *Treasury of Knitting Patterns* and *Second Treasury of Knitting Patterns* (Scribners, USA).

BOOKS ON HISTORY OF KNITTING AND TRADITIONS

Bush, Nancy, *Folk Knitting in Estonia* (Interweave Press, 1999).
Gravelle LeCount, Cynthia, *Andean Folk Knitting* (Dos Tejedoras Fiber Arts Publications, 1990).
Hinchcliffe, Frances, *Knit One, Purl One; Historic and Contemporary Knitting from the V & A's Collection* (Precision Press, London).
McGregor, Sheila, *Traditional Fairisle Knitting* (Batsford, 1981).
McGregor, Sheila, *Traditional Scandinavian Knitting* (Batsford, 1983).
Pearson, Michael, *Traditional Knitting* (Collins, 1984).
Rutt, Richard, *A History of Handknitting* (Batsford, 1987).
Thompson, Gladys, *Guernsey and Jersey Patterns* (Batsford, 1969).

SUPPLIERS AND INFORMATION FOR COURSES

SUPPLIERS

Texere Yarns
College Mill
Barkerend Road
Bradford
West Yorkshire
BD3 9AQ
Website: www.texereyarns.co.uk
(a range of dyed and undyed yarns, wool, cottons, linens, silks and synthetics).

George Weil and Fibrecrafts
Old Portsmouth Road
Peasmarsh
Guildford
Surrey GU3 1LZ
Website: www.fibrecrafts.com
(all sorts of textiles supplies: yarns including knitting wire, dyes, books and textile craft magazines, including USA publications).

Rowan and Jaeger Yarns
Green Lane Mill
Holmfirth
West Yorkshire
HD7 1RW

COURSES

For information about handspun yarn, lectures and workshops in weaving and knitting, contact:

The Association of Guilds of Weavers, Spinners and Dyers: there are regional branches in each county in the UK.
Website: www.wsd.org.uk

The Knitting and Crochet Guild
Website: www.knitting-and-crochet-guild.org.uk

COLLEGES

Urchfont Manor
Urchfont
Devizes
Wiltshire SN10 4RG

West Dean College
West Dean
Chichester
West Sussex PO18 0QZ
Website: www.westdean.org.uk

INDEX